DISCOVERING
RUNES

DISCOVERING
RUNES

Bob Oswald

CHARTWELL
BOOKS, INC.

Published in 2008 by
CHARTWELL BOOKS, INC.
A division of BOOK SALES, INC.
114 Northfield Avenue
Edison, New Jersey 08837
USA

**Copyright © 2008 Regency
House Publishing Limited**
Niall House
24–26 Boulton Road
Stevenage, Hertfordshire
SG1 4QX, UK

For all editorial enquiries, please contact
Regency House Publishing at
www.regencyhousepublishing.com

ISBN-13: 978-0-7858-2400-8

ISBN-10: 0-7858-2400-6

Printed in China

TO HELEN
How Love came in, I do not know,
Whether by th'eye, or ear, or no;
Or whether with the soul it came,
At first, infused with the same;
Whether in part 'tis here or there,
Or, like the soul, whole every where.
This troubles me; but I as well
As any other, this can tell;
That when from hence she does depart,
The outlet then is from the heart.
OF LOVE BY ROBERT HERRICK

CAUTION: Runes are a fascinating subject, primarily because of their antiquity and use as an ancient writing system. Many people down the ages have ascribed magic powers to them, while just as many believe the opposite to be true. The information in this book has been written and should be used only with good intentions in mind, and must on no account be used for negative or harmful purposes.

CONTENTS

CHAPTER ONE
THE ORIGINS OF THE RUNES – 12

CHAPTER TWO
DIVINATION WITH RUNES – 34

CHAPTER THREE
INTERPRETING THE RUNES – 54

CHAPTER FOUR
DOWSING WITH THE RUNIC PENDULUM – 170

CHAPTER FIVE
BINDRUNES – 182

CHAPTER SIX
GANDR MAGIC – 204

CHAPTER SEVEN
RUNE TRANSCRIPTION – 222

BIBLIOGRAPHY – 238

INDEX – 242

PREFACE

Discovering Runes deals with the aspects of the subject that seem to be of most interest to my website visitors and correspondents from around the world. It is not intended to be a comprehensive guide to all matters runic.

You will find that divination with runes is well-covered in Chapter 2, but the rest of the book concentrates on those areas of runic knowledge where I have developed some expertise over the last 50 years or so, and for which I have gained a little recognition.

Much of the content will be new to many readers, and I hope that even those who are experienced in the use of runes will discover something they didn't know before.

Dowsing with the runic pendulum, the construction and use of bindrunes, the use of the runic gandr, and writing with runes, are subjects that have not been discussed in any great detail by the most popular writers, and my intention is to offer my own methods and ideas on these specialist topics as a useful contribution to the body of published work.

Many people have helped and contributed to the publication of the book and I should like to acknowledge some of them here. First and most importantly, my wife Helen and my son Rob for their faith, support and patience during the writing; my daughter Sarah for her advice and assistance on the structure of the book; my good friend and colleague Mark Porter for his input and development work on the subject of pendulum dowsing; the people at Regency House for their guidance and perseverance with the project; and last but never least, Freya Aswynn for her unstinting encouragement and advice on all matters runic. Thank you all, I couldn't have done it without you.

Finally, just in case there is any doubt, all errors and omissions in the content or structure of the work are entirely my own responsibility. They are not attributable to any of the above-mentioned.

Bob Oswald
Buckinghamshire, England

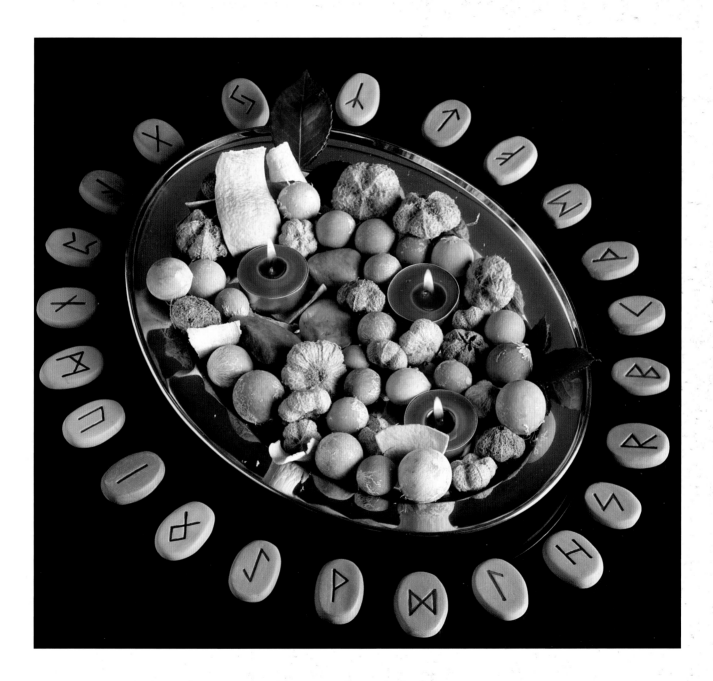

THE ORIGINS OF
THE RUNES

CHAPTER ONE
THE ORIGINS OF THE RUNES

HISTORY AND CONJECTURE

No one knows exactly how old the runes are, but rune-like symbols appeared as cave markings as early as the late Bronze Age (circa 1300 BC). They are mentioned in the Bible, but their use as oracles to be consulted most probably pre-dates their use as a system of writing.

The following exploration of their early history is riddled with 'probables' and 'possibles' through lack of reliable documentation and very little archaeological evidence. But from the few clues that do exist I have pieced

together my own ideas about how divining with runes, and later, writing with runes, came about.

If we move on from the late Bronze Age another 500 years to about 800 BC we find a nation called Scythia beginning to emerge. Its people were a mix of Asian, and perhaps even North African tribes, who plundered and pillaged their way towards Europe, establishing a dominant kingdom. It was founded in the Caucasus region to the north of the Black Sea and

12

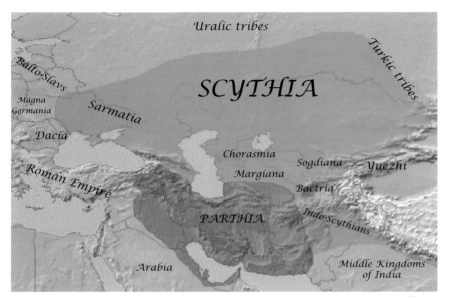

SCYTHIA

Uralic tribes

Turkic tribes

Balto-Slavs

Magna Germania

Sarmatia

Dacia

Roman Empire

Chorasmia

Margiana

Sogdiana

Bactria

Yuezhi

Indo-Scythians

PARTHIA

Arabia

Middle Kingdoms of India

The fact that each of the runes were given meaningful names confirms they had some magical or religious significance to their users as well as being an alphabet used for records and messages. The word rune itself comes from the old Norse word *runa*, meaning a secret or mystery, which suggests that the early runemasters and

OPPOSITE ABOVE: The hällristningar (rock carvings) of Sweden provide evidence of settlements from about 3,000 years ago. Shown here are pictograms of animals.

OPPOSITE BELOW: A copy of writings found on the walls of a cave, thought to have been influential in the development of the runic alphabet.

ABOVE: Map showing the approximate extent of the Scythian nation from 800 BC to AD 200.

RIGHT: Statue of the Greek historian Herodotus.

eventually came to straddle the divide between Asia and Europe. By 100 BC it had reached as far as the eastern edge of modern Germany.

Back to the timeline and another jump of 400 years takes us to the Greek historian Herodotus (484–424 BC), who tells of a form of divining with wooden sticks used by Scythian tribesmen c. 470 BC. He describes the ceremony as intensely ritualistic and mentions the use of soporific smoke. This method of divination probably drove northwards with the spread of the Scythian people, reaching their Germanic neighbours through trade and social interaction.

runemistresses were considered to have brought some magic or mystic power to their understanding of the runes.

As for the runic alphabet used for writing messages and inscriptions, there are those who suggest that many of the rune forms were copied from Roman script – the system of letters on which modern Western writing is based. Such examples as Mannaz (M), Fehu (F), Berkanan (B), Raido (R) are obviously very similar, but it is more likely that the rune symbols were developed independently, probably earlier, and probably from the same sources as Roman script.

The most plausible theory, however, is that runic script developed from the Etruscan alphabet. Etruria was a pre-

LEFT: The Kylver Stone, dating from around AD 400, is the earliest Futhark inscription, found in Gotland in 1903.

BELOW: An early map of Etruria.

OPPOSITE ABOVE: Runes from around AD 1070, from Bergen, Norway, their lines running across the grain of the wood.

OPPOSITE BELOW: Cornelius Tacitus.

Roman kingdom that ranged along the western side of the Italian peninsula, rstretching all the way north to the high Alps and reaching its apogee during the 6th and 7th centuries BC. At the same time as the Germanic tribes of the north were interacting with the Scythians, so their more southerly compatriots were in contact with the Etruscans. They were trading across the Alps that divided their two nations and it would be logical to assume that the written script of the more advanced Etruscans migrated with traders to form the basis of the runic alphabet. Certainly there are similarities between Etruscan and runic characters, and I can only surmise that they became blended over the centuries with the existing Bronze Age magic symbols; perhaps that is why the runes served as both a written

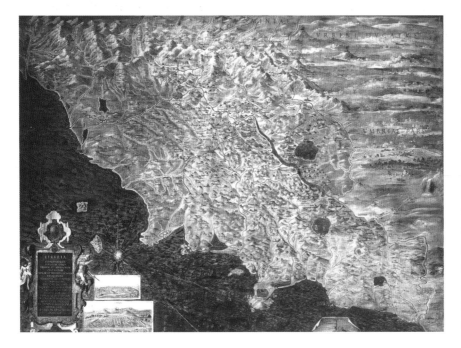

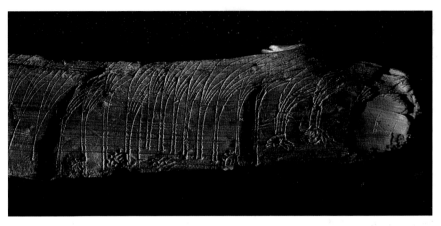

script and as symbolic representations used in practical magic.

Looking at the needs of an ancient rune-user wishing to mark runes, he would require nothing more that a stick of wood and a sharp knife to incise the marks. Both of these requisites would have been available to man from the very earliest times and I am convinced that such magical applications as divination would have arisen long before there was any need for writing messages.

Moving on to the 1st century AD we find the Roman historian, Cornelius Tacitus (c. 58–120), recording a

Germanic tribal ritual in some detail in Chapter 10 of his ethnographical work, *Germania*. This was written c. AD 97, when Tacitus was consul to that region of the Roman Empire, and may well predate the emergence of the runic alphabet or Futhark as a system of writing. He wrote:

To the use of lots and auguries, they are addicted beyond all other nations. Their method of divining by lots is exceedingly simple. From a tree which bears fruit they cut a twig, and divide it into small pieces. These they distinguish by so many several marks, and throw them at random and without order upon a white garment. Then the Priest of the community, if for the public the lots are consulted, or the father of a family about a private concern, after he has solemnly invoked the Gods, with eyes lifted up to

heaven, takes up every piece thrice, and having done thus forms a judgment according to the marks before made.

Tacitus uses the Latin word *auspiciis*, meaning consultations with the gods which, in the above passage is translated as auguries. To me this reads very much like a divining session, and there are similarities between the description by Tacitus and the Scythian method recorded by Herodotus. Bearing in mind the contact made between northern Germanic people and Scythians some 600 years before, I feel it is beyond coincidence that the two methods should have so much in common. Tacitus neither describes the several marks on the small pieces nor does he mention runes as such, but what other marks would these Germanic people have used?

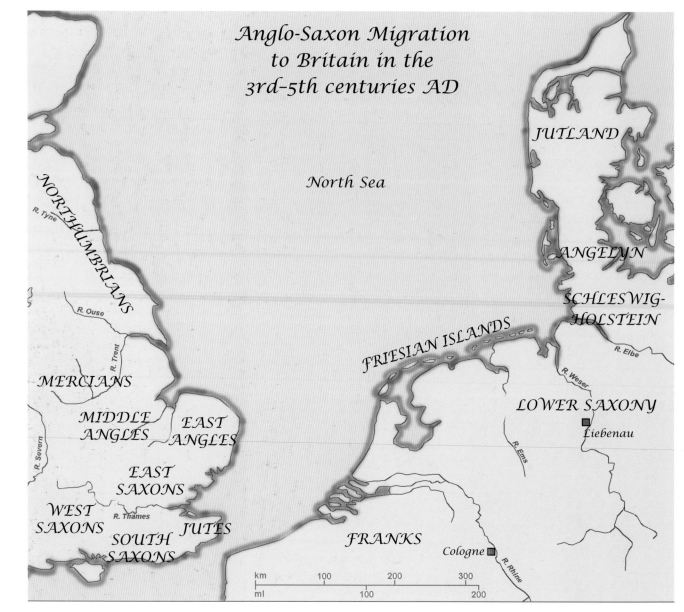

Anglo-Saxon Migration
to Britain in the
3rd–5th centuries AD

North Sea

JUTLAND

ANGELYN

SCHLESWIG-
HOLSTEIN

R. Elbe

NORTHUMBRIANS

R. Tyne

R. Ouse

R. Trent

FRIESIAN ISLANDS

R. Weser

LOWER SAXONY

MERCIANS

MIDDLE
ANGLES

EAST
ANGLES

R. Ems

Liebenau

R. Severn

EAST
SAXONS

WEST
SAXONS

R. Thames

JUTES

SOUTH
SAXONS

FRANKS

Cologne

R. Rhine

km   100   200   300

ml   100   200

Tacitus has been accused of dwelling on the vices and vagaries of peoples whom he considered to be uncivilized, including the Germanic tribes. His motivation may not always have been to record factual data for history, but to point the finger at practices he considered barbaric. Whatever his motives, his description seems to fit consultations with runic oracles.

There is little doubt that the runes were initially cut into wood, their very shapes confirming this by the avoidance of the horizontal or curved line. If you experiment with a flat wooden surface you will find that it is easy to cut lines straight across the grain, or at an angle to it, because the broken fibres do not heal, thus the cuts stay visible for as long as

the wood survives. But it is much more difficult to cut a curve with a straight knife blade, and it is almost impossible to cut a line in the same direction as the grain because very few fibres will be cut. Thus the incision closes up as the wood dries out, and the line disappears. There would be little benefit in carving a message that could not be read a few hours later.

OPPOSITE: Map showing the migration of rune-users from continental Europe to Anglo-Saxon Britain.

LEFT: The Tarot card, representing the Hanged Man, is presumed to equate with Odin's self-inflicted ordeal, when he hung on the World Tree for nine days and nights.

BELOW LEFT: The Anglo-Saxon form of the Hagalaz rune.

BELOW: Bragi the Skald with his wife Iduna. Bragi was the Norse god of poetry and a famed raconteur.

A selection of modern runestones, made from wood, ceramic and crystal.

The earliest discovered inscriptions using the runic alphabet date from around AD 150 and, if my guesswork is correct, suggest that the art of runic divination was widespread in northern Europe from a much earlier date. There are 24 runes in the original alphabet, which is called the Elder Futhark. It became known as the Futhark or Futhorc, after the names of the first 6 runes: Fehu, Uruz, Thurisaz, Ansuz, Raido and Kauno, the third rune, Thurisaz, making the TH sound on its own. The runes represent objects, gods, people, animals, concepts and occurrences. They are known by names from which their alphabetic values were taken, but in view of the above theory it would seem likely that the Germanic and Norse tribes, which developed them, had ascribed names and meanings to many of the runes long before there was any need for a written language.

There are very few surviving runic inscriptions and most of them are on stone or metal, being the most durable of materials. Only a handful of inscriptions carved on wood have ever been found.

There is sufficient evidence to show that the Anglo-Saxon Runes (known to runologists as the Anglo-Friesian Runes

because of their geographical occurrence)
are the same 24 basic runes, with
variations in their form due to their usage
over the centuries.

For example, the Hagalaz of the
Norsemen resembled an angled H, but the
Anglo-Saxons added a second cross-bar.
Variations in pronunciation also occur:
the Norsemen, for instance, pronounced
W as V, but lazy Anglo-Saxon tongues
had adapted this to the modern W sound
by AD 600. A guide to the probable
Anglo-Saxon pronunciations is given in
Chapter 7.

Recorded history abounds with
examples of runes being endowed with

DISCOVERING RUNES

secret or mystical power. The ancient Prose Edda has Odin hanging on Yggdrasil, the World Tree (located at the centre of the universe and joining the nine worlds of Norse cosmology), in order to gain knowledge of the runes and the wisdom of kingship, an event often equated with the Tarot's Hanged Man. Here Bragi, the Norse god of poetry and master of the skalds (minstrels) is also

mentioned, who reputedly had runes tattooed on his tongue, presumably giving him his magical gift of eloquence.

The later saga, Erik the Red, describes a runemistress in full regalia, while the Finnish Kalevala, as recorded by Lönnrot in 1835, tells of a confrontation by wizards, when runic songs were used to cause fire and devastation.

OPPOSITE & LEFT: Runestones in and around the town of Sigtuna, in Uppland, Sweden, dating back to the 9th century.

LEFT: The lid of the Franks Casket shows Egil the Archer defending his stronghold.

BELOW: The casket's back panel, showing Titus, the Roman general, conquering and destroying Jerusalem in AD 70.

Some modern experts claim that stones were commonly used in divination, but I have found no evidence of this despite extensive research. Many different styles and materials are now used to make rune sets for divining, but all the indications, whether from runology, known pagan religious beliefs, or Saxon witchcraft ritual, point to the use of wood, particularly from fruit-bearing trees.

In order to re-create the traditional ancient methods accurately, I make rune sets from wood such as blackthorn, ash, beech, birch, chestnut, elder, hawthorn, hazel, juniper, lime, rowan, sycamore, willow and a few other woods from wild trees. In keeping with the pagan respect for the environment, I never cut wood from living trees, but use windfall or forested branches.

RUNIC RELICS AND MONUMENTS

Having mentioned the scarcity of archaeological finds, I feel it is appropriate to mention the few that have contributed to our sparse knowledge on the subject. Virtually all the information we have concerning the use of runes in ancient times comes from the study of relics and monuments bearing runic inscriptions. In the following few paragraphs and illustrations I have chosen some of the most interesting and influential items.

THE FRANKS CASKET

Perhaps Britain's most important runic relic, now in the British Museum, London, is the little box known as the Franks Casket, named after Sir Augustus Franks, who brought it (or at least most of it) back to Britain in the 19th century. All but one side of the casket was retrieved by him from a French farm, where it was being used as a workbox, the other side having been acquired by an Italian collector and which is now in Florence.

The box is made of whalebone and is exquisitely carved on all its surfaces. It dates from the 7th century and tells its stories in both runic and Roman scripts. Its original silver clasp and corner posts are unfortunately missing. The casket's front panel depicts a scene from the tale of Wayland the Smith and a single Christian image, the Adoration of the Magi, with the word MAGI, written as Mannaz-Ansuz-Gebo-Isa, just above the three kings and to the left of the Star of the East.

Wayland, also known as Weland, Volundr, Volund or Vulcan, was the most important smith-god of Norse and Anglo-Saxon mythology. With his brothers and King Didung, he features in the exciting poem, The Lay of Volund, or *Völundarkvida*, from the Icelandic Poetic Edda.

The lid of the casket (opposite above) has a scene showing Egil, together with his wife, the valkyrie Alruna, enclosed in a castle keep, with Egil shooting arrows at numerous attacking forces; I suspect that the full story of this event has been lost in the intervening centuries. Egil, Aegli or Ægli, a brother of Wayland the Smith, was also a great archer, and there is a tale about him, approximating to the story of William Tell, in the Saga of Thidrik (Deitrich in German).

The left side of the casket shows Romulus and Remus being suckled by the she-wolf, while the right features another lost legend of a horse named Hos, sitting on a 'Sorrow Mound', and tells how the whale, from whose bone the casket was made, was found beached after a storm.

The back (opposite below) has a scene showing the Roman general, Titus (later to be emperor), conquering and destroying Jerusalem in AD 70.

The language used, other than runic, is Northumbrian Anglo-Saxon, which places the casket's origin in Yorkshire,

LEFT & OPPOSITE: The Jarlabanke Runestones, Jarlabanke's Bridge, Uppland, Sweden, number about 20 from the 11th century, inscribed in Old Norse with the Younger Futhark. They appear to have been commissioned by the chieftain of a clan at Täby, named Jarlabanke Ingefastsson. On several of the runestones he states that he is a Christian rather than a pagan.

The so-called Jarlabanke's Bridge is a causeway at Täby, which was originally bordered by four runestones and many raised stones.

PAGE 28: Wayland's Smithy is one of many prehistoric sites associated with Wayland, the Norse and Anglo-Saxon god of blacksmithing and metalworking. It is one of the most impressive and atmospheric Neolithic long barrows in Britain.

Durham or Northumberland in the north of England.

Unconnected with the Franks Casket, but interesting nonetheless, is the fact that there is a Neolithic burial chamber, named Wayland's Smithy, situated in the Vale of the White Horse, Oxfordshire, in England. A local legend has it that anyone whose horse casts a shoe may leave the animal at the smithy overnight, together with a small silver coin, where, on returning in the morning, they will find that the horse has been re-shod and the money gone.

Another local tale tells how Wayland had a lazy and useless apprentice called Flibbertigibbet. Wayland, thoroughly exasperated, eventually picked the boy up and hurled him as far as he could, down

into the valley, where Flibbertigibbet landed in a meadow and was turned to stone. This stone became a boundary marker and remains to this day in a field known as Snivelling Corner.

THE GREAT STONES OF JELLING

Jelling, in North Jutland, Denmark, is the site of two great tumuli and two great stones, covered with runic inscriptions, the larger having been raised by King Gorm, and the smaller by Harold I (Harold Bluetooth), who also erected a Christian church on the spot. The inscription, dating from around AD 960–965, reads: 'King Haraldr ordered this monument to be made in memory of his father Gormr and his mother Thorvi.

This was Haraldr who won all Denmark for himself and for Norway, and who made the Danes Christian.'

CUNEBALD'S CROSS

This is a 5th-century runic monument from Lancaster, England. The inscription reads: 'Gebiddeth fora Cyunibalth Cuthbereng', which may be translated as 'Pray-ye for [the soul of] Cunebald Cuthbertson'. The 3-ft (10-m) cross, found in 1807, is now in the British Museum, where the drawing on page 30 was made.

LEFT: Gorm's Stone, Jelling, Denmark.

ABOVE: Harold Bluetooth's Stone.

THE ORIGINS OF THE RUNES

RUNIC CALENDARS

Also known as runic almanacs, they seem to have been medieval Swedish inventions, written on parchment or carved onto staves of wood, bone, or horn. The earliest is the Nyköping staff, dating from around the 13th century.

CONTINUOUS STAVE INSCRIPTIONS

The way we write modern English is from left to right, but the old rune-carvers were not so particular, and there are many examples of writing from right to left, and a few of 'continuous stave' writing, which is writing left to right on the first line then right to left on the next, and so on, making the passage continuous but reversing the direction on every line. Some inscriptions were coloured in with paint to make them more visible, and there is archaeological evidence that red, white and black pigments were used.

THE ISTABY STONE AT BLEKINGE

This 7th-century memorial is the oldest surviving Danish runestone, even though Blekinge is now a part of Sweden. The inscription reads: 'In memory of

Hariwolfafr. Hathuwolfafr, son of Haeruwulfafr, cut these runes.'

Blekinge is an important runic site, with four stones that make reference to runic magic and the use of charms. Archaeological runologists view them with some scepticism, claiming that the indications are confused and incomprehensible. I personally find nothing confusing or incomprehensible about 'He who breaks these stones will suffer by the hidden forces of rune magic'. Despite the professed disbelief of the academics, it should be noted that the stones still stand unmolested after the passage of 13 centuries.

HILDDIGUTH'S STONE

The pillow stone from a nun's grave in Hartlepool, Co. Durham, England, dated from around AD 650. Measuring about 8 x 6in (20 x 15cm), it was discovered in 1833. It bears only the nun's name, which is a forerunner of the modern 'Hilda'.

FAR LEFT: Detail of a drawing made from Cunebald's Cross.

BELOW LEFT: The Istaby Stone is the oldest surviving Danish runestone.

A TWAY-STAVED INSCRIPTION

This 6th-century fragment of a cross or grave pillar from Falstone, Northumberland, is inscribed with both Roman lettering and runic symbols. The inscription may be translated: 'Eomar set this memorial after Hroetbert his uncle. Pray-ye for his soul.'

HROSSKETILL'S STONE

This is a fragment of a cross from Braddan, Isle of Man. The full story of this memorial is lost, and only the villain of the piece is identified. The inscription reads: '. . . and Hrossketill under trust betrayed a man sworn to him by oath.'

The Isle of Man was the earliest Viking settlement of Britain, but given names on memorials show that, even as early as AD 500, intermarriages between Celtic Britons and Norsemen were becoming common.

LEFT: A line drawing of an object bearing a tway-staved inscription in both runes and Roman lettering.

BELOW LEFT: Hilddiguth's Stone, taken from a nun's grave.

BELOW: A fraction of a Celtic cross, featuring part of a story relating to Hrossketill's treachery.

DIVINATION
WITH RUNES

CHAPTER TWO
DIVINATION WITH RUNES

SUITABLE SUBJECTS FOR RUNIC DIVINATION

It is important to remember that the runes are not a method of general prediction. They cannot foresee the future course of world events or in any way pre-ordain things to come. They are more a way of focusing psychic energy to better understand a person's present situation, the way in which it may be affected in order to achieve a desired outcome, and a way of determining that person's destiny. Thus, the subject's future, as determined by his or her own actions and own personality, may be made clearer through the runes.

Some things are more appropriate to divination than others. You may wish to have advice on the timing of an action, your conduct, relationships, decision-making, or business matters. These are issues rather than questions. The runes will answer questions, but the answer you get will depend upon your own frame of mind at that point in time. It is more effective to state an issue and let the runes make comment on it. This will give you an appraisal of the whole issue and the reasons for the cast, rather than a simple 'yes' or 'no' answer.

For example, you might say, 'The issue is my relationship with John', instead of asking the narrower question, 'Does John love me?' Our role in the process is just as important as that of the runes themselves. If you do no more than look for 'yes' or 'no' answers, then you are not taking an active part. But by invoking the wider issues you are giving the runes an opportunity to react to your psyche and thus provide a fuller response.

There are occasions when the response made does not appear to fit the issue raised. This can happen when the runes have chosen to address a more serious issue than the one posed. This may be because the more serious issue ultimately will control the lesser issue you originally raised. This can be useful if you cannot decide which of several issues to work on. The runes will decide for you, and the response will clearly indicate the matter requiring the more immediate attention.

PREPARING FOR THE DIVINING SESSION

There are no formal rules for consulting

LEFT: Candlelight creates an atmosphere conducive to divining.

OPPOSITE: The runes may give advice on relationships, both present and future.

the runes. Some prefer morning, others evening: it is purely a matter of personal preference. You should try and find a time and place where the distractions of everyday life do not intrude. Keep light to a minimum; draw the curtains if it is during the day. I find candlelight the most conducive. Relax as much as possible, make yourself comfortable, and try to focus your mind on the subject of the consultation before casting begins. If there are others present they should be in accord with your thoughts and aspirations, for confusing answers will result if two minds are concentrating on different issues.

Familiarity is an important factor as far as the runes are concerned. They will be more responsive when handled by a single person, when kept in the same place, and when cast in the same manner every time. The best rune sets for divination are boxes holding the runestones within a bag. It is also a good idea to use the same cloth or table covering (the field) when casting, and to carry it with the runes when travelling to another place. Ancient tradition would have a white cloth, but any colour apart from black would be suitable.

It is quite acceptable to begin the session with no preamble, although many rune-casters prefer to perform some formal ritual to assist them (and the runes) in achieving the fine focus required for the best results. An invocation or a short prayer would be appropriate. You will find details of several books in the bibliography which give examples of invocations and prayers.

Norse gods, such as Odin, Freya, Tiw, Ing, or even Loki the Trickster, may be called, but I would refrain from invoking Thor, the god of thunder, who has the reputation for being vengeful and unforgiving.

For initial guidance, the early Norse gods are detailed briefly in the *Larousse Encyclopaedia of Mythology*, available in most library reference sections. My personal habit is to call upon the Sun and Moon to guide the runes towards truth and light.

RUNE SPREADS AND RUNE CASTS
The basic difference between the two divining systems is quite simple: in a rune

OPPOSITE: An illustration of Wotan (Odin) and Brünhilde, from Richard Wagner's opera, The Valkyrie.

RIGHT: Freya, the Norse goddess of love, beauty and fertility, from a 1902 illustration by H.J. Ford.

Invoke the Sun and the Moon to guide the runes towards truth and light.

spread you select the runes for the reading from a hidden cache, placing them in a pattern to be read according to their positions relative to one another. In a rune cast you throw or drop the runes so that they fall randomly onto the field, reading them according to their location upon it.

Another major difference is in the method of interpretation. With a rune spread it is common to use reverse and sometimes converse interpretations for many runes. For example, Berkanan upright can mean growth, whereas

Berkanan reversed (upside-down) can indicate shrinkage or lack of growth, while Berkanan converse (face-down) can mean hidden growth. With a rune spread, therefore, it is a simple matter to place the drawn rune onto the casting surface in exactly the same aspect as it came to hand.

But it is obviously impractical in a rune cast to take these alternative interpretations into account, because the runes can fall at any angle. With a random pattern like this, it would be altogether too restrictive to limit the interpretation to individual runes, and it would also curtail some of the more complex and subtle relationships going on between the neighbouring runes in the cast.

DEVELOPING YOUR OWN DIVINING METHOD

It is important that you adopt a method that suits you and provides useful results. If you feel the need for a more disciplined method than a random cast, construct your own casting field on a paper or cloth, or even on a marked diagram on the ground. Choose a format that has significance for you, rather than accepting a predefined pattern, such as those described below.

If you feel a little out of your depth using the full rune set, for your first efforts select only a few, starting with only 3, 4, or 5 runestones to get the feel of the rune-cast method, then progressing to 8, 9 or 12. This will provide enough depth for meaningful readings, and the runes themselves will help you decide how they wish to be read.

With experiment and practice you will develop your own rune-casting method that works with your rune set and your own psyche. Once you have found a system that works for you, stick to it. Consistency in method is one of the keys to successful divining.

RUNE CASTS

THE GERMANIA CAST Take all of the runes in your hands and cast them on the surface of the field. You can throw the runes gently, or you can let them fall from your hands from a height of about 8–12in (20–30cm).

Discount any runes that fall beyond the perimeter of your casting surface and, without looking at them, choose three at random. Once you have the chosen three, set them down in a row and interpret them according to the rules of the 3-rune spread (page 43).

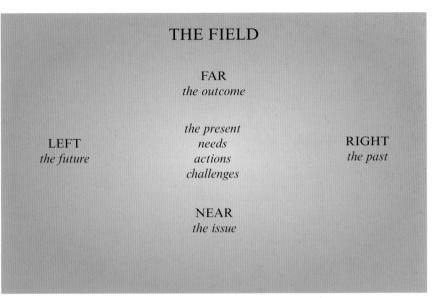

THE FIELD

FAR
the outcome

the present
LEFT   *needs*   **RIGHT**
the future   *actions*   *the past*
challenges

NEAR
the issue

THE 9-RUNE CAST For a detailed overview of a situation, or an examination of your spiritual path, pick nine runes unseen from the rune bag and hold them in both hands while you formulate your question. Then throw or let the runes fall onto your casting surface. Face-up runes relate to the current situation and the circumstances which led to it. Those near the centre are more relevant than those at the periphery.

Runes close together or touching one another complement each other or represent a single concept, while those at opposite ends of the casting surface represent opposing influences. Occasionally, a rune will land completely off the casting surface, in which case you should disregard it completely.

Once you have considered the face-up runes, turn over the others without changing their relative positions. (Personally, at this point, I find it useful temporarily to turn over the face-up runes, so that I can concentrate on the now-revealed face-down ones.) These face-down runes represent external and/or future influences, thus pointing to possible outcomes.

You must decide for yourself how the relative positions of the runes affect the cast. When you have performed a number of casts, and have decided on meanings for various positions or patterns, you will be able to formulate your own conventions for interpreting your rune cast in future. It is important to be consistent in your interpretations, so once you find the meaning for a form or pattern that fits your situation, always try to keep to the same interpretation in the future. But don't be too restrictive in setting rules. In other words, you should not be tempted to see every triangle or square as a set pattern that must mean the same thing every time.

Rune-casting is a very subjective practice that depends as much on your mindset as it does on the runes themselves, so be open-minded and ready to reassess your own judgement from time to time.

RUNE SPREADS
The field (see above left) on which you spread the runes represents the world in which you live. To the Right represents the past, and to the Left the future. When reading horizontally (right-to-left), the central area represents the present.

On the vertical axis, closest to you, Near represents the issue, while Far represents the outcome of the issue. The central area, when read in this direction, represents your needs, your actions and the challenges which may effect them.

ᚠ ᚢ ᚦ ᚨ ᚱ ᚲ ᚷ ᚹ
ᚾ ᚺ ᛁ ᛃ ᛇ ᛈ ᛉ ᛊ
ᛏ ᛒ ᛖ ᛗ ᛚ ᛜ ᛞ ᛗ

The red runes are reversible. They look the same and have the same meaning right-way-up or upside-down.

down or face-up) may make a difference to the meaning.

The nine of the runes read the same upright or reversed, but the other fifteen do not. For example, Ehwaz upright looks like M, but reversed looks like W.

Place the field on the surface before you. Take the runes from their box and place them unseen in the bag. Swirl the runes in the bag gently around, using your writing hand, and let a rune fall naturally into your fingers. Feel it and sense whether it is the right one to draw. Most commonly a feeling of 'rightness' will be experienced, and less commonly you may feel a tingle in the fingers, a sense of warmth, sometimes a shiver or movement of the rune itself.

Draw the runes one at a time and place them on the field. Never turn the runes, but place them exactly as they come to hand on the field. Whether they are upright or reversed (i.e. upside-down or right-way-up), and whether they appear converse or obverse (i.e. face-

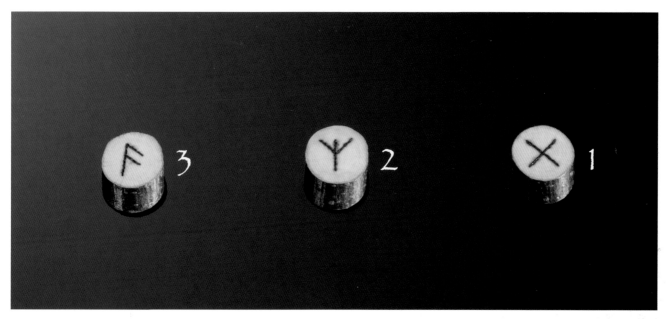

When placing the runes on the field you most often work from Right to Left, then from Near to Far. For example, if placing a 3-rune spread, you would lay Right, Centre, then Left.

If placing a 5-rune spread you would lay Right, Centre, Left, Near, Far. And if placing a 6-rune spread you would lay Right, Near Centre, Left, Near, Far Centre, Far.

THE TRADITIONAL RUNE SPREADS
ODIN'S RUNE For an overview of an entire situation, state the issue aloud and draw a single rune. The rune drawn will encompass the entire matter from past to future, actions and outcome. This is particularly useful when there is a critical matter for which you seek instant guidance.

THE 3-RUNE SPREAD With the issue stated aloud, draw three runes and place them Right, Centre and Left.
• The first rune (Right) speaks of the situation as it now is.
• The second (Centre) suggests the course of action called for.
• The third rune (Left) foretells the outcome resulting from that action.

Alternatively, if you are seeking to remove an obstacle from your life or your progress, you may read the runes: Right – myself at present. Centre – the challenge or obstacle, and Left – the best possible outcome if I am able to overcome the obstacle. As to the matter of how to remove the obstacle for a satisfactory outcome – a supplementary spread of Odin's Rune may provide the answer you need.

The 3-rune spread.

43

THE RUNIC CROSS This is a 6-rune spread which will give you an in-depth analysis of an issue. It is similar to the classic Tarot layout, and is probably derived from that source. The layout is also very similar to the shape of the Celtic Cross, which was a common motif in northern Europe even in pre-Christian times. So who can say with any certainty which came first?

The Tarot is reputed to have originated in ancient Egypt, but there is no evidence to link it with Bronze Age Europe. It is possible that the two similar methods of divination developed independently, but historians are quite adamant that new-age users developed the Runic Cross idea from the Tarot method as late as the 20th century, and I would not argue the point. Whatever its origins, it is a useful method.

State the issue and draw six runes in the manner stated above. Spread them Right, Near Centre, Left, Near, Far Centre, Far.

OPPOSITE: The Runic Cross.

RIGHT: The Quest for Truth Spread.

PAGES 46-47: The Ardboe Cross does not bear runes but it is in a similar tradition.

• The Right rune represents the past, the situation that has brought this issue to exist.
• The Near Centre represents you now.
• The Left is what lies ahead of you.
• The Near gives the underlying basis of the issue, often subconscious or unrecognized reasons why the position has arisen.
• The Far Centre represents the nature of the obstacles or blockages you wish to overcome.

• The Far rune (known as the Outcome) foretells the best outcome you can anticipate if overcoming the challenge.

THE QUEST FOR TRUTH SPREAD This spread will provide the most detailed analysis of personal destiny. It must be undertaken by an experienced rune-caster on behalf of the questioner. The spread requires the selection of nine runes: one by the caster, the other eight by the questioner.

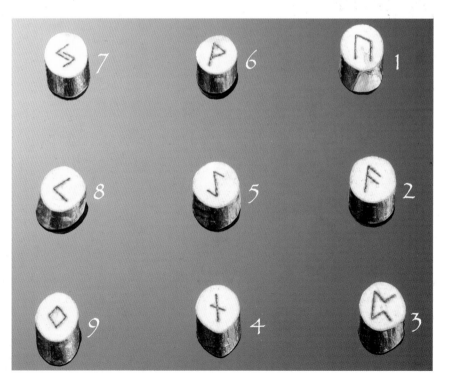

The Three Lifetimes Spread.

The caster should spend some time in the company and in conversation with the questioner to get a feel for the person and the subject. Then the caster will select a single rune in the usual way which will represent the questioner, who will then take the rune bag and select eight more runes, one by one, laying them in a three-by-three square to the pattern shown in the diagram on page 45.

• The top right rune (drawn by the caster) representing the questioner, also known as the Significator, a term borrowed from the Tarot.

• The second rune reveals the inner self and is spread middle row right.

• The third rune is spread bottom row right and deals with the goals or ideals of the questioner.

• The fourth rune is spread bottom row middle to represent the past.

• The fifth rune is spread at the centre of the square and tells of family matters.

• The sixth rune is spread top row middle and deals with the questioner's health.

• The seventh rune is spread top row left and speaks of religious matters.

• The eighth rune is spread middle row left and represents the questioner's friends.

• The ninth and final rune is spread bottom row left and reveals the final outcome.

THE THREE LIFETIMES SPREAD This spread is dedicated to reincarnation, and should not be practised lightly. It gives a three-level insight into your journey through this life, your previous existence, and any future incarnation you may expect. If practising this spread, you should be aware that not everyone will experience reincarnation, and it is perhaps better not to know one way or the other.

Many diviners have found this method to give startling results, often invoking long-forgotten memories and on occasion causing the questioner some discomfiture.

Speak the issue and draw five runes in the same manner as before.

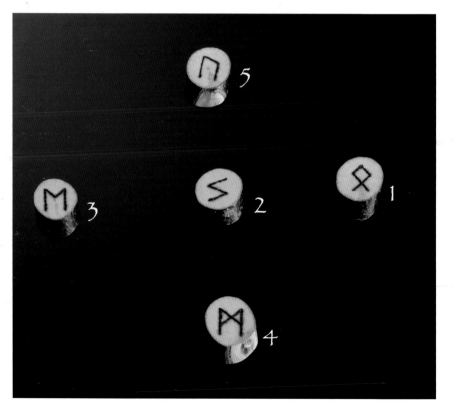

Spread them Right, Centre, Left, Near, Far.

• Right represents your birth and childhood and will point out your talents, attributes and shortcomings.

• Centre represents your present life and will indicate actions you must take to improve your present life and thus deserve another.

• Left shows what your future in this life holds for you if you follow the advice given.

• Near gives an indication of your past life, its character and your behaviour. And finally, Far gives an indication of (a) whether you will reincarnate and (b) if so, what kind of person you will be.

THE FIVE DIRECTIONS SPREAD This spread is representative of the four cardinal compass points and is useful when dealing with questions about position or location, such as a missing person or object, the objective of a journey, the right place for some kind of action or performance, even perhaps where to live if you are moving house.

When stating the issue the caster should specify the place and, if required, details of the object or person being sought.

• The first rune is placed at the near

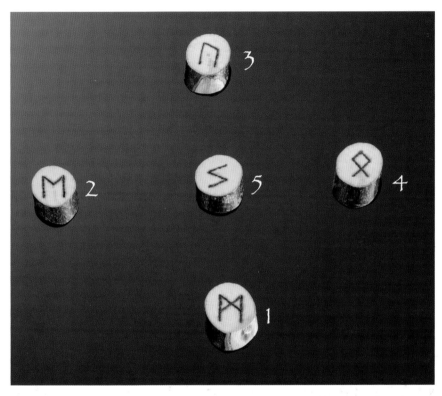

point at the end of the cross and tells of the existing circumstances and influences that cause the present situation.

• The second rune is laid to the left and represents obstacles and challenges that need to be overcome.

• The third rune is laid at the top of the cross at the far point and shows any benefits and positive omens accruing from the portent of the spread.

• The fourth rune is laid to the right and sums up the outcome of the enquiry. It may simply be a positive or a negative indication, telling whether the spread has been a success or a failure.

• The fifth and final rune, laid at the centre of the cross, will tell of the overall situation and how the future might unfold.

The Five Directions spread.

The Thor's Hammer Spread This spread is about self-discovery and is a solitary exercise. It is a personal thing to be undertaken by the individual rather than with a questioner and a caster.

• The first rune is laid at the near point of the hammer and is read 'how others see me' and should be interpreted as the persona you present to others.

• The second is laid above and to the left of the first rune. It is read 'my fears' and points at the things that worry you most.

• The third is laid above and to the right of the first rune and is read 'what I seek'. This will reveal to you what your overall aim in life is – or has been – as it is buried in your subconscious mind.

• The fourth rune is laid on the centre line of the field above this first rune and is read 'my best approach', pointing to the positive actions you should take towards your objectives.

• The fifth rune is laid above the fourth at the centre point of the field. This one is read 'my goal' and will identify the next prime objective you should strive for in pursuit of your ambitions.

• The sixth rune is laid directly above the fifth on the centre line of the field. This one is read 'obstacles to overcome' and will point at major problems that stand in your way.

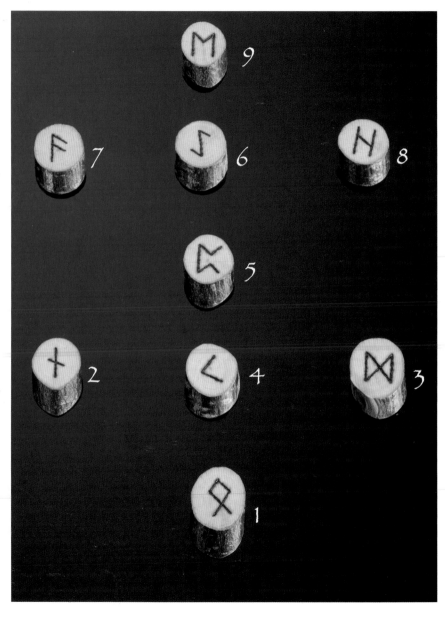

• The seventh rune is laid above and to the left of the sixth and is read 'my destiny'. This will show the outcome of the progression towards you life ambition as it stands now.

• The eight rune is laid above and to the right of the sixth. This rune will identify any alternative direction you could take should your present path prove less than satisfactory. Perhaps it will even indicate an alternative goal for you to aim at and is read 'the way to my real self'.

• And finally the ninth rune is laid on the centre line at the top of the field. This is read 'my real self' and will strip away all pretension revealing your persona, not as seen by yourself or by others around you, but in its true colours.

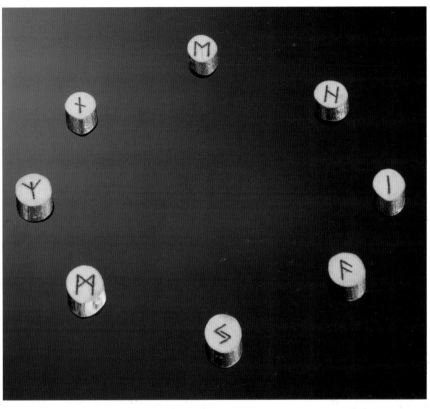

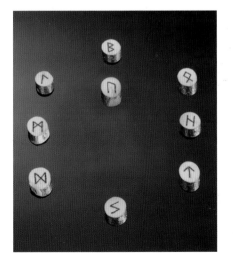

There are other forms of rune spread that I have not explored in this book, such as the Eightfold Wheel, which has been borrowed from Buddhism by modern Wiccans and New Age rune-users.

The Nine Worlds of Yggdrasil is another modern spread system that is worthy of mention, but it is too complex for a full description to be given here. The developments by Freya Aswynn have enabled advanced rune-users to relate their explorations to the Nine Worlds of Norse mythology. The layout for the spread is shown here.

OPPOSITE: Thor's Hammer Spread.

ABOVE: The Eightfold Wheel Spread.

LEFT: Nine Worlds of Yggdrasil Spread.

INTERPRETING
THE RUNES

CHAPTER THREE
INTERPRETING THE RUNES

We can never be sure exactly how these names were pronounced by the various tribes and peoples who used them, nor the precise sounds the runes represent. However, the sounds of personal names, place names, and some words which are still in English use today, can be estimated with some accuracy. Moreover, the study of runic inscriptions on memorials and gravestones, which have survived, has to some extent allowed runologists to reconstruct Anglo-Saxon pronunciations.

The Bewcastle Cross, shown here, and the Tway-Staved cross fragment (see page 31) are good examples of useful inscriptions. The Bewcastle Cross, incidentally, with its reference to Oswald, King of Northumbria (AD 605–642), was my first introduction to

The remains of the Bewcastle Cross in Cumbria, England, with its weathered runic inscriptions.

BASIC MEANINGS OF THE RUNE NAMES

RUNE	NAME	LETTER	LITERAL EQUIVALENT	MEANING
ᚠ	Fehu	F	Cattle	Money, Wealth
ᚢ	Uruz	U	Wild Ox	Strength, Health, Virility
ᚦ	Thurisaz	Th	Giant	Frost Giant, Chaos, Demon, Devil
ᚨ	Ansuz	A	Odin, Messenger	Odin, a Message, Source, A Leader
ᚱ	Raido	R	Riding, Wagon	A Journey, Riding, Arrival, Transport
ᚲ	Kauno	K	Wound, Torch	Enlightenment, Transition, Light
ᚷ	Gebo	G	Gift	Gift, Love, Windfall, Surprise
ᚹ	Wunjo	W	Joy	Joy, Happiness, Romance
ᚺ	Hagalaz	H	Hail	Disruption, Adversity
ᚾ	Naudiz	N	Need	Need, Necessity, Extremity
ᛁ	Isa	I (short)	Ice	Stagnation, Cold, Stability
ᛃ	Jera	J	Year	The Harvest, A Cycle, Success
ᛇ	Ihwaz	I (long)	Yew Tree	Bow or Weapon, Defence
ᛈ	Perth	P	Uncertain (Dice Cup?)	Chance, Gamble, Science, Technology
ᛉ	Algiz	Z (Rr)	Uncertain (Pine woods?)	Protection, Shelter
ᛊ	Sowilo	S	Sun	Light, Energy, Victory, Wholeness
ᛏ	Tiwaz	T	The God Tiw	A Warrior, Diplomacy, Courage
ᛒ	Berkanan	B	Birch Twig	Fertility, Growth
ᛗ	Ehwaz	E	Horse	Speed, Progression, Loyalty
ᛘ	Mannaz	M	Man	The Self, Humanity
ᛚ	Laguz	L	Water	Sea, Flow, Direction
ᛜ	Ingwaz	Ng	Angel, The God Ing	Harmony, Unity, Peace
ᛟ	Othila	O	Hereditary Land	Birthright, Possessions, Home, Family
ᛞ	Dagaz	Dj	Day	Breakthrough, New Dawn, Transformation

the subject of runes. I would like to think the great king is an ancestor of mine, but sadly it's rather unlikely, Oswald being a common enough family name in England's north-east. It was most probably a name taken by warriors who fought for the king, or possibly by monks, who were permitted to marry and had families in ancient times, and who served in abbeys dedicated to the king after he was canonized a saint.

Runic correspondence with the sounds produced in modern English, and shown in the table on page 225 in Chapter 7, is only approximate, but certain runes are worthy of special attention:

Ansuz   Long A as in father or perhaps OA as in board. This later became an O and a new A rune was introduced.

Thurisaz   TH as in think.

Gebo   A guttural G as in Scottish loch.

Wunjo   Either W as in wild or V as in vest.

Ihwaz   I as in nice.

Algiz   Early Norse tribes pronounced this Z as in zoo. Anglo-Saxons changed this to a rolling R with the tongue beating on the roof of the mouth as found in Scottish and Breton dialects.

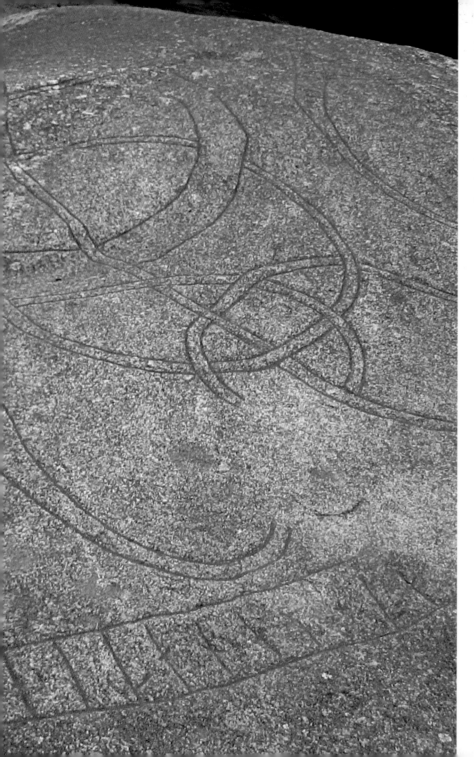

The Granby Runestone (Swedish: Granbyhällen) is the largest runic inscription in Uppland, Sweden. It was made in memory of a father, a mother and some other people. The father Finnvid's property is also mentioned.

Ingwaz   This was possibly a glottal stop
         sound, but may be taken as NG
         as in either finger or sing.

Jera   Y as in year.

On the following pages you will find
fuller interpretations of the runes. These
are intended for your guidance while
learning how to use them, but do not
attempt to find the answers to any serious
life-changing questions until you have
learned more of the art through practice
and training or further reading.

Obviously there are thorough
examinations of these meanings in many
published works, some of which I mention
in the bibliography. There are also a
number of journals covering runic matters,
and you will doubtless encounter
runemasters and runemistresses, who will
help you gain a deeper understanding of
the runes and how to interpret them.

CONVERSE AND REVERSE MEANINGS

When a rune is cast obverse (i.e. face-up),
it indicates that the matter is (or will
become) clear to you, is straight-forward
or honest.

When runes are cast converse (i.e.
face-down) it indicates that the matter told
by the rune may be withheld from you,
kept secret, hidden from view, or that it
may be dishonest.

When runes are cast upright (i.e. the
symbol is right-way-up) the representation
is of the true meaning of the rune.

When runes are cast reverse (i.e. the
symbol is upside-down) this suggests
negative aspects of the matter, or that it
may be unwise to do something.

For example, Berkanan represents
growth when cast upright, but when
reversed might indicate the absence of
growth, a reduction in stature, or may
warn against the concept of growth.

When runes are cast both converse
and reverse, take both alternative
interpretations into account in your
reading. Once again using converse and

reverse Berkanan as the example, this
would indicate absence of growth, or
reduction of stature, which is hidden from
you, or is dishonest in nature; theft from a
store of goods or money would be a case
in point.

The blank is not really a rune at all,
but is a quite modern invention, not used

*ABOVE: A prehistoric cave painting of an
aurochs, a now-extinct ox, in Lascaux,
France.*

*OPPOSITE: The birch tree is associated
with the Berkanan rune.*

by the ancients and not accepted by traditionalists. I personally do not use the blank in casting, but for those who prefer to include it, the following should be noted.

If you intend using the blank you might like to note that its persistent emergence in any aspect may be taken as an indication that the matter is not open to interpretation by the runes. If you find that a series of casts throw up the blank consistently, then the issue should be either re-stated more clearly, re-cast without the blank, or left alone.

Many rune-casters take the blank as a death warning, but this should not be taken seriously. In the context of a rune cast or spread it indicates the demise of an ideal or an endeavour, rather than an actual physical death.

SOME NOTES ON INTERPRETATIONS AND ASSOCIATIONS

The runes featured here are from the Elder Futhark and from the Anglo-Friesian Futhark, the forerunner of the Anglo-Saxon runes later used throughout Britain. I have not included the nine later runes, added by rune-carvers in the Northumbria region of Britain from around AD 700, but hopefully I shall get around to doing that one day.

INTERPRETING THE RUNES

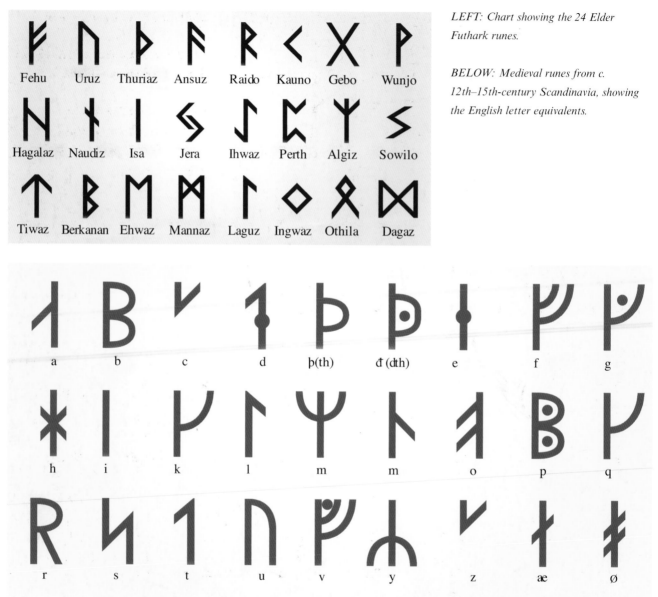

Fehu	Uruz	Thuriaz	Ansuz	Raido	Kauno	Gebo	Wunjo
Hagalaz	Naudiz	Isa	Jera	Ihwaz	Perth	Algiz	Sowilo
Tiwaz	Berkanan	Ehwaz	Mannaz	Laguz	Ingwaz	Othila	Dagaz

LEFT: Chart showing the 24 Elder Futhark runes.

BELOW: Medieval runes from c. 12th–15th-century Scandinavia, showing the English letter equivalents.

a	b	c	d	þ(th)	ð(dth)	e	f	g
h	i	k	l	m	m	o	p	q
r	s	t	u	v	y	z	ae	ø

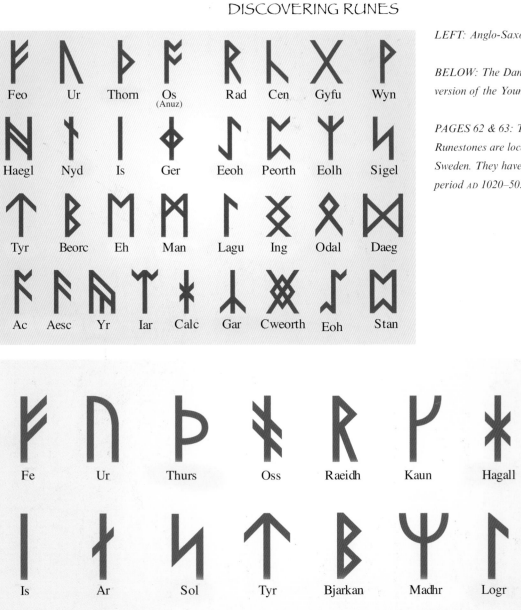

Feo	Ur	Thorn	Os (Anuz)	Rad	Cen	Gyfu	Wyn
Haegl	Nyd	Is	Ger	Eeoh	Peorth	Eolh	Sigel
Tyr	Beorc	Eh	Man	Lagu	Ing	Odal	Daeg
Ac	Aesc	Yr	Iar	Calc	Gar	Cweorth	Eoh	Stan

LEFT: Anglo-Saxon Futhorc runes.

BELOW: The Danish c. 9th–12th-century version of the Younger Futhark.

PAGES 62 & 63: The Broby bro Runestones are located in Uppland, Sweden. They have been dated to the period AD 1020–50.

Fe	Ur	Thurs	Oss	Raeidh	Kaun	Hagall	Naudhr
Is	Ar	Sol	Tyr	Bjarkan	Madhr	Logr	Yr

61

In the meantime, wherever you see the term 'Anglo-Saxon' mentioned, I am referring to the runes that first appeared in Britain, probably in the 3rd century AD. Archaeological runologists call these the 'Anglo-Friesian' runes because they were also in use in Friesia, a region of the Netherlands now known as West Friesland.

The runes all have names that were significant to the ancient Germanic tribes, Norsemen and Anglo-Saxon pagans who used them. Some were named for gods, like Ing and Tiw; some for animals and plants, like the aurochs (an extinct European ox) or a birch twig; some for natural features, such as a lake, hail or ice; some for everyday objects used by the ancients, e.g. a wagon or chariot or an archer's bow; and some for timeless concepts, like joy, a gift, and humanity.

The rune meanings are augmented by further interpretations for upright (right-way-up), reverse (upside-down) and converse (face-down) presentation, and all these meanings and interpretations are detailed in the following pages.

The runes were given names by the ancients who used them, which could be those of the gods, objects in everyday use, and the animals or the natural features, colours and elements surrounding them.

The runes are traditionally associated with gemstones or crystals, trees, plants or herbs, colours, and the elements. Sometimes these associations are instantly obvious. For example Berkanan, the rune of growth and fertility, is associated with the fast-growing birch tree, its colour being dark-green, as are its leaves; its element is Earth, from which the tree springs.

Less obvious is Berkanan's herbal association with lady's mantle or dewcup (*Alchemilla vulgaris*). But a good

herbalist will tell you that it is also connected with fertility and is regarded as a woman's best friend, in that it regulates periods and clears inflammations of the female reproductive organs.

Berkanan's association with the moonstone (also known as wolf's eye, fish's eye or water opal), with the strange, shimmering light that it emits, is due to the gem's supposed ability to promote growth and maintain high energy levels in its wearer.

FEHU

THE RUNE OF WEALTH & FULFILMENT

NAMES AND MEANINGS

Anglo-Friesian/Germanic: Fehu

Norse (Viking): Fe

Old English: Feoh

Other Names/Spellings: Faihu, Fé, Feh, Feo

Pronunciation: Fay-who

English Letter Equivalent: F as in fat

Translation: Cattle, money, wealth

Meaning: Reward, wealth, nourishment

CHARACTERISTICS

Realized ambition, good health, wealth, love fulfilled, good fortune. But remember to be charitable and show compassion for others.

Fehu means cattle, a measure of wealth to the ancients. Today Fehu means movable wealth, such as money and

Moss agate, the nettle, the elder tree, cattle and Frey, the Norse god of fertility, are all associated with the rune Fehu.

possessions. It also implies the energy and hard work that leads to wealth. Fehu can also mean emotional and spiritual riches, as well as money.

PERSONAL INTERPRETATION

Fehu is Frey's rune, and he is the god of fertility, itself a form of wealth. It is a rune of unselfish abundance. Let it shine forth to lighten your path and the paths of others. Your spiritual richness will never be diminished, but don't waste it on those who will abuse it. Discernment is important.

Reverse: Failed ambition, health problems, poverty, unrequited love, bad luck.

Converse: Hidden reward, undiscovered wealth, nourishment withheld.

ASSOCIATIONS

Runic Number:	1
Colour:	Light Red
Gemstone:	Moss Agate
Tree:	Elder

Herb or Plant: Nettle

Element: Fire and Earth

Polarity: Female

Associated gods: Frey, Freya

Astrological Correspondence: Aries

THE RUNE POEM

Verse I Fehu

Wealth is a consolation to all men

Yet much of it must each man give away

If glory he desire

To gain before his god.

URUZ

THE RUNE OF STRENGTH

NAMES AND MEANINGS

Anglo-Friesian/Germanic: Uruz

Norse (Viking): Ur

Old English: Ur

Other Names/Spellings: Uraz, Urs, Urur, Urus

Pronunciation: Oor-ooze

English Letter Equivalent: Short U as in under, OO as in booze

Translation: aurochs, the giant wild ox of Europe and Asia (now extinct)

Meaning: Physical or mental strength, health. For a man – male virility, manhood. For a woman – fertility, femininity, womanhood

CHARACTERISTICS

Terminations, new beginnings, an opportunity disguised as a threat, mental agility, physical development, mental and bodily health, power.

Uruz means aurochs, the Eurasian wild ox, the last of which became extinct in Poland in 1627. Uruz encompasses physical strength, endurance, courage, and the raw, wild power of freedom. It includes emotional and spiritual strength, male sexual potency, and good health. It can also imply a challenge leading to a major life change.

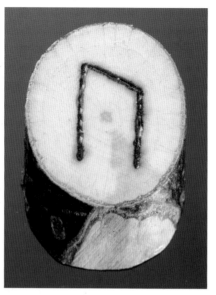

PERSONAL INTERPRETATION

You have the strength within you to fulfil all your dreams, but with strength comes responsibility. Strength is not a force to wield over others, but one to stop others exerting power over you. Use your strength to keep focused on your path and to prevent yourself from being outmanoeuvred. There will always be negative people, but don't let them upset you. Master your own ego and you will succeed.

Reverse: Failure to think clearly, ill-health or lack of mental fortitude. Beware showing signs of weakness, also of threats to your person or position.

Converse: Hidden strengths must be realized. Shun apparent opportunities, the signs are deceptive.

ASSOCIATIONS

Runic Number:	2
Colour:	Dark Green
Gemstone:	Carbuncle (cabochon-cut Red Garnet)
Tree:	Birch
Herb or Plant:	Iceland Moss
Element:	Earth
Polarity:	Male
Associated gods:	Thor, Urd

Astrological Correspondence: Taurus

THE RUNE POEM

Verse II Uruz

The Aurochs is fearless and huge of horn

A ferocious beast, it fights with its horns

A famous moor-stalker that:

A mettlesome wight.

The rune Uruz has associations with the

aurochs, Icelandic moss, the birch tree and

a zodiacal affinity with Taurus the Bull.

made by the dwarves Brokk and Eitri. Mjöllnir was able to hit any object at which Thor threw it, when it would return to his hand. Thor used his hammer many times in battle against the evil frost giants, the harbingers of chaos.

Mjöllnir also carved out three valleys in a mountain near Utgard when Thor threw his hammer at Loki the Trickster, who was disguised as a giant and was using the mountain as a shield.

Thor will carry his mighty hammer into the final battle of Ragnarok, where he will use it to crush the head of the world serpent Jormungand, but Thor will

be poisoned by the mighty serpent and die after taking nine steps.

This will not be the end of Mjöllnir, however; the hammer will be passed along to Thor's two sons to defend the world to come after Ragnarok.

Most Norsemen, especially sailors and warriors, wore a Mjöllnir amulet as protection against enemies and foul weather, and to give them courage. Sailors and warriors were invariably the same, acting as oarsmen in the Viking galley ships and as infantry in battle.

THURISAZ
THE RUNE OF CHAOS, EVIL & TEMPTATION
NAMES AND MEANINGS
Anglo-Friesian/Germanic: Thurisaz
Norse (Viking): Thurs
Old English: Thorn
Other Names/Spellings: Thuith, Thurisa, Thurisar, Thorunisaz, Thyth
Pronunciation: Thoor-ee-sawz
English Letter Equivalent: TH diphthong, as in thin or in weather
Translation: Giant, monster, devil, a thorn, the god Thor or his hammer, Mjöllnir

According to Viking legend Mjöllnir was Thor's magical golden hammer,

Thor, his magic hammer, Mjöllnir, sapphires, house leeks (sempervivums) and the blackthorn (sloe) are some of the elements connected with the rune Thurisaz.

MEANING

Magical power, the forces of chaos or of evil, temptation. A warning.

CHARACTERISTICS

Threats from persons of power or position. Resist temptations which offer reward through dishonesty or trickery. Heed the omen of dishonour or physical harm.

The energy of Thurisaz can be used for good or for chaos. It represents the forces of the human psyche, including anger and lust. The thorn is a symbolic weapon, in that it can pierce, stab or tear. But it can also be protective, like a thorny hedge. Thurisaz may also signify a stroke of luck, but is more often a warning that luck is is beginning to run out.

PERSONAL INTERPRETATION

You have the power within you to face anything. Fear nothing, for you have the authority to claim your destiny. Let no one deter you from your search for the truth. Spiritual authority brings power, and it is up to you to use that power in an unselfish and loving way. Power can corrupt if you do not have a true and honest heart.

Reverse: Evil may be overcome. An omen of good. An exhortation to proceed.

The danger is slight.

Converse: The evil will be hidden or may appear disguised as good.

ASSOCIATIONS

Runic Number:	3
Colour:	Bright Red
Gemstone:	Sapphire
Tree:	Blackthorn
Herb or Plant:	House Leek
Element:	Fire

Polarity:	Male
Associated god:	Thor
Astrological Correspondence:	Mars

THE RUNE POEM

Verse III Thurisaz

The Thorn is sorely sharp for any thane
Hurtful to hold
Uncommonly severe
To every man who lies among them.

ANSUZ

ODIN'S RUNE, THE MESSENGER RUNE

NAMES AND MEANINGS

Anglo-Friesian/Germanic: Ansuz

Norse (Viking): Ass

Old English: Os

Other names/spellings: Aesir, Ansur, Ansus, As, Aza, Easc, Oss

Pronunciation: Awn-sooze

English Letter Equivalent: A as is hat. Long A as in harm, lawn

Translation: A god, a leader, Odin (in reverse Loki, messenger of the gods and a trickster)

Meaning: Knowledge, wisdom. Communication, the mouth, a message, eloquence

CHARACTERISTICS

Ansuz is primarily Odin's rune and represents communication, creativity, controlled and divine power. Spiritually, it is the rune of prophecy and revelation. It also encompasses the ideas of wisdom, knowledge, reason, and therefore of instruction and good advice. It might also refer to a test, examination, or perhaps an interview. It can mean a letter, book, paper, message or other information.

Because Loki was a renowned trickster, Ansuz reversed may also portend a surprise, trick or subterfuge.

PERSONAL INTERPRETATION

The answers to questions are available but not yet recognized. Look for signs and confirmations which are all around you. Everything has significance and appreciation of this will lead to understanding. Ensure you don't ignore the message because you don't like the content. All experience is a lesson that teaches by acknowledging the truth,

*Ansuz has associations with the ash tree and the fly agaric fungus (*Amanita muscaria*).*

OPPOSITE: The Birth of Venus, 1879, by William Bouguereau.

when knowledge and wisdom will increase.

Reverse: Take care not to misinterpret information. Something you read is more important than it appears. Beware of pranks.

Converse: Failed communication, lack of clarity or awareness, hidden messages, secrets, information disguised. What appears to be a trick is genuine.

ASSOCIATIONS

Runic Number:	4
Colour:	Dark Blue
Gemstone:	Emerald
Tree:	Ash
Herb or Plant:	Fly Agaric
Element:	Air
Polarity:	Male
Associated gods:	Odin, Eostre, in reverse Loki
Astrological Correspondence:	Venus

THE RUNE POEM

Verse IV Ansuz

The Mouth is the source of every speech,
The mainstay of wisdom,
And solace of sages,
And the happiness and hope of every eorl.

RAIDO

The Traveller's Rune

NAMES AND MEANINGS

Anglo-Friesian/Germanic: Raido

Norse (Viking): Reid

Old English: Rad

Other Names/Spellings: Radh, Raidha, Raidho, Raidu, Reda, Reidr, Reidh, Reidthr

Pronunciation: Rye-doh

English Letter Equivalent: R as in red

Translation: Riding, a journey

Meaning: A journey, arrival, departure, union or re-union. Events concerning travel or vehicles

CHARACTERISTICS

Travel is indicated. New friends or old friends return. Jobs are connected with transport or overseas locations.

Raido can mean wheel, ride, or travel, but it also has a deeper meaning. Riding a horse includes both movement and direction. A journey can be long and arduous, requiring planning, foresight, determination, and fortitude. Raido can therefore refer to the journey of life (the wheel of life), or to a spiritual quest. It might also mean transport or communication, such as delivering or receiving a message.

PERSONAL INTERPRETATION

Recognize that everything comes in cycles and that by recognizing this you will progress quickly and efficiently. Align your lifestyle with the seasons and honour the turning of the year. Embrace hard times, knowing that the harder it is now, the easier it will get in the future.

Everything has its opposite, and challenges bring equal and opposite rewards.

Reverse: Stagnation, lack of movement or change, isolation, mechanical breakdown or failure to arrive. A missed deadline.

Converse: Meetings take an unexpected course. A secret mission. Home-based jobs. An enemy disguised as a friend.

ASSOCIATIONS

Runic Number:	5
Colour:	Bright Red
Gemstone:	Chrysophase
Tree:	Oak
Herb or Plant:	Mugwort
Element:	Air
Polarity:	Male
Associated gods:	Ing, Nerthus
Astrological Correspondence:	Sagittarius

THE RUNE POEM

Verse V Raido

For every hero in the hall is Harness soft
And very hard for him who sits astride
A stout steed
Over miles of road.

The zodiac sign of Sagittarius the Archer,
mugwort (wormwood) and the mighty oak
are associated with the rune Raido.

KAUNO

THE RUNE OF FIRE, THE TORCH OF ENLIGHTENMENT

NAMES AND MEANINGS

Anglo-Friesian/Germanic: Kauno

Norse (Viking): Kaunaz, Kaun

Old English: Ken, Cen

Other Names/Spellings: Chozma, Kano, Kauna, Kaunan, Kaunaz, Kenaz, Kusmas

Pronunciation: Cow-noh

English Letter Equivalent: Hard C as in cat. K as in king

Translation: A firebrand or torch. In some (doubtful) translations, an ulcer, wound or an opening

Meaning: Heat, light, enlightenment

Possibly mistaken: burning, an opening, ulcer or injury and thus mental anguish.

The original meaning of the name Kauno is 'firebrand' or 'torch', but at some stage the meanings 'wound', 'sore', 'ulcer' or 'opening' appear to have crept

in, possibly because of the shape of the Elder Futhark version.

These later meanings are reflected in the Norse and Icelandic rune poems, but it should be remembered that these are more recent than the Anglo-Saxon poem (see the verse opposite).

I have never been too happy with the wound-ulcer-sore interpretation of Kauno. I think there is a possibility of mistranslation by historians and poets of the past, and I suspect that these Kauno meanings have that same mistaken origin.

The Germanic root word Ken produces a whole family of words in modern European languages, all of them related to knowledge, understanding, or 'knowing' in the biblical sense of a carnal relationship. I can see the correlation between these and the 'torch of enlightenment', but the relationship between the torch as the cause of a burn and the wound-ulcer-sore interpretation is just a little too contrived for my taste. I leave you to make up your own mind.

CHARACTERISTICS

Kauno's main significance is related to fire, light, warmth, enlightenment and knowledge. It sheds light on the path, dispels the dark shadows of ignorance, and helps us to see with true discernment. It suggests that understanding must lead to action, and light in the darkness implies spiritual illumination. Kauno also represents the natural warmth and companionship of hearth and home and thus good health.

In its rather suspect 'ulcer' translation it can represent a doorway or portal leading from darkness into light.

The cowslip, the bloodstone, the Norse goddess Freya, and the pine tree are associated with the rune Kauno.

PERSONAL INTERPRETATION

You are gaining a new understanding of life and its meaning. New insights await, but don't be complacent. Use this new understanding or it will be worthless. Look for ways to use your insights for the good of yourself and others. Enlightenment is replenishable. The more you use, the more knowledge you gain. Enlightenment itself is not the goal, it is just the starting point of a great adventure that will show you deep wisdom and understanding as long as you proceed with truth and honesty.

Reverse: Cold, darkness, lack of knowledge or insight.

Converse: Beware hidden danger. What appears to be the true path may be a false trail. Something dark or cold may conceal great energy.

ASSOCIATIONS

Runic Number:	6
Colour:	Light Red
Gemstone:	Bloodstone
Tree:	Pine
Herb or Plant:	Cowslip
Element:	Fire
Polarity:	Female
Associated gods:	Heimdall, Freya, Frey

Astrological Correspondence: Venus

THE RUNE POEM

Verse VI Kauno

A Torch alight is known to all alive
Brilliant and bright,
It burns most oft
Where Aethlings rest themselves within.

GEBO

THE RUNE OF A GIFT, LOVE & FORGIVENESS

NAMES AND MEANINGS

Anglo-Friesian/Germanic: Gebo

Norse (Viking): Gyfu

Old English: Gyfu

Other Names/Spellings: Gebu, Geuua, Geofu, Giba, Gifu, Gipt, Giof, Gjof

Pronunciation: Ghay-bow

English Letter Equivalent: G as is good Gh as in the CH of Scottish dialect as heard in loch, but softer

Translation: Gift

Meaning: Love, partnership. Forgiveness. A gift, talent, skill or ability

CHARACTERISTICS

Ask forgiveness and it will be given. A gift, present or windfall is foretold. Discovery or development of a skill or talent. Artistic or musical ability. Show compassion. Be not afraid to declare love. Good fortune in partnerships.

Gebo, rune number 7, is the origin of our 'lucky seven' superstition. It represents a gift, whether it be a present, an attribute, a certain skill or ability. Perhaps the greatest gift of all is to give or to receive. To the ancients, a gift always called for another in return, so accepting a gift places you under an obligation to the giver, the gods, destiny, another person. Gebo can also mean a partnership or union, either in business or in love. Or it can mean forgiveness. Gebo is commonly used as the sign for a kiss, the outward show of affection.

PERSONAL INTERPRETATION

A gift presents you with the choice of acceptance or rejection. If you accept you must be prepared to give in return. Everything has its price, but with spiritual

*The zodiac sign of Pisces the Fish, the heartsease (*Viola tricolor*), the opal, the gift of love and the elm tree are some of Gebo's affinities.*

DISCOVERING RUNES

Reverse: Gebo has no reverse.

Converse: Personal animosity, particularly from partners. Hidden talents need uncovering. Think again about romance.

ASSOCIATIONS

Runic Number:	7
Colour:	Dark Blue
Gemstone:	Opal
Tree:	Elm
Herb or Plant:	Heartsease
Element:	Air
Polarity:	Male & Female

Associated gods: Odin, Gefjon

Astrological Correspondence: Pisces

THE RUNE POEM

Verse VII Gebo

Generosity in men is to honour and praise
And dignity a prop;
And for every wrack,
Riches and substance, who has naught else.

gifts the cost is always worth it in the end. You must find the balance between giving and receiving, while learning to give responsibly. This means deciding when to give and to whom, remembering that it is inappropriate to give without discrimination.

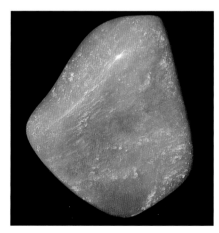

WUNJO

THE RUNE OF JOY

NAMES AND MEANINGS

Anglo-Friesian/Germanic: Wunjo

Norse (Viking): Wyn

Old English: Wyn

Other Names/Spellings: Vend, Vin, Uinne, Winja, Wungo, Wunja, Wunju

Pronunciation: Vun-yoh

English Letter Equivalent: W as in wax. V as in van

Translation: Joy

Meaning: Happiness, light, emotional satisfaction

CHARACTERISTICS

Understanding, realization of ambition, success in romance, good health. Partnerships flourish. New beginnings are blessed with joyfulness. Your eyes are opened to the truth. Wunjo is linked with a reward, a feeling of goodness and satisfaction, peaceful winning, and ultimate achievement. It contains the idea of everything going well because you are in total harmony with life.

Wunjo also implies close cooperation and companionship with other people, because joy is not usually a solitary emotion. When so much of life can be negative, it is important to allow Wunjo's joy to reach into every part of your life.

PERSONAL INTERPRETATION

Happiness is yours if you are willing to work for it. You must strive for balance and harmony in your life. Always look for solutions rather than dwell on problems. For happiness to last, it must be founded on truth and honesty. Hide from the truth and you hide from true happiness. Seek only what is good and right, and good fortune cannot fail to follow.

Reverse: Misunderstanding, ambition stalled, romantic or partnership

difficulties. Not a good time for new ventures.

Converse: The truth is hidden from you. Success is elusive but work hard. Imagined love is false. Partnerships under strain through secretive behaviour.

ASSOCIATIONS

Runic Number: 8
Colour: Light   Blue
Gemstone: Diamond
Tree: Ash
Herb or Plant: Flax
Element: Ice (i.e. Water)
Polarity: Male
Associated gods: Odin, Frigg
Astrological Correspondence: Leo

THE RUNE POEM
Verse VIII Wunjo
He enjoys Delight who knows little of
woe,
Of suffering and sorrow,
And has for his own prosperity, pleasure,
Eke the plenty of cities.

Flax (linseed), the ash tree and ice are
some of Wunjo's associations.

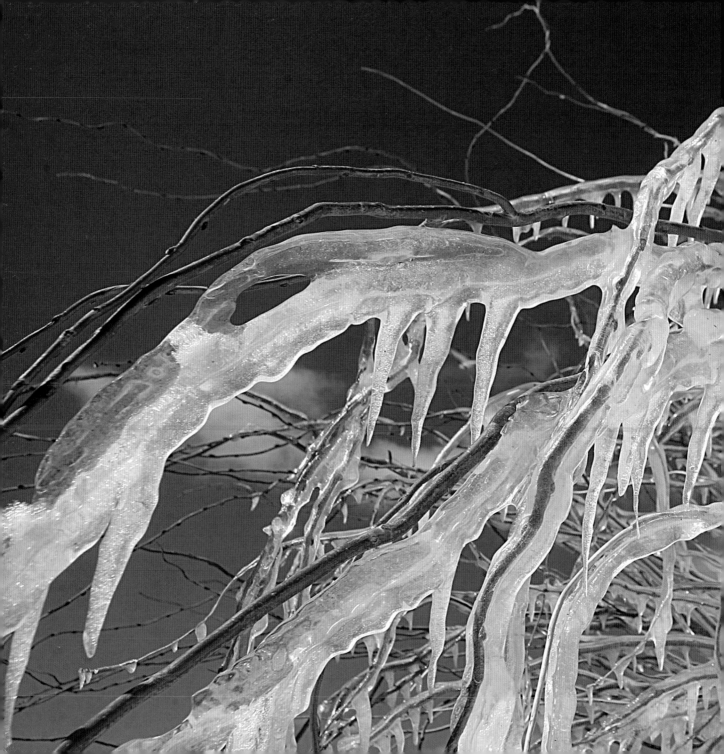

HAGALAZ

THE RUNE OF DISRUPTION

NAMES AND MEANINGS

Anglo-Friesian/Germanic: Hagalaz

Norse (Viking): Hagall

Old English: Haegl or Ghaegl

Other Names/Spellings: Haal, Hagalar, Hagl, Hagalz, Haglaz

Pronunciation: Har-ghawl-arz

English Letter Equivalent: H as in hat

Translation: Hail

Meaning: Weather, damaging natural forces, disruption, interference

CHARACTERISTICS

The weather is a significant factor; insure against damage from storm, flood or

hailstorm may be daunting, but if you catch a hailstone you will see that it is only water and nothing to be feared. So it is with challenges: fire up your determination and face these head-on, knowing they are only stepping-stones on the way to your goal. The greater the challenge the more you gain by overcoming it.

lightning. Prepare for disruptive influences. A third party interferes with relationships.

Hagalaz represents hail, and what it may portend may be likened to an unexpected hailstorm, being an elemental disruption in your life. When Hagalaz is linked with other runes, it can suggest limitation, interruption or delay, implying a complete change in direction. Hagalaz can also mean suffering, hardship, illness or injury.

PERSONAL INTERPRETATION

Challenges are occurring in your life which must be faced rather than feared. A

Reverse: Hagalaz has no reverse.

Converse: Hidden dangers from the natural world. Apparently easy tasks hide unexpected dangers. A lover or partner is hiding something.

ASSOCIATIONS

Runic Number: 9
Colour: Light Blue
Gemstone: Onyx
Tree: Ash
Herb or Plant: Bryony
Element: Ice (i.e. Water)
Polarity: Female
Associated gods: Urd (of the Norn sisters), Heimdall
Astrological Correspondence: Aquarius

THE RUNE POEM

Verse IX Hagalaz
Hail is the whitest of grain
Whirled from heaven's height,
The wind hurls it in showers
Into water then it turns.

*The ash tree, bryony (*Brionia*), the zodiac sign of Aquarius the Water-Carrier and the elemental forces of nature are associated with the rune Hagalaz.*

NAUDIZ

The Rune of Necessity

Names and Meanings

Anglo-Friesian/Germanic: Naudiz

Norse (Viking): Naudr, Nauthiz

Old English: Nyd

Other Names/Spellings: Naud, Naudhr, Naudir, Naudth, Nauths, Nied, Noicz

Pronunciation: Now-dthiz

English Letter Equivalent: N as in now

Translation: Need, extremity

Meaning: Need, want, craving. demand, deprivation, compulsion, desire

Characteristics

Control your emotions. Do not succumb to cravings. Your health is at risk,

Snakeroot (Ageratina), the lapis lazuli, the element fire and the rowan tree are some of the rune Naudiz's associations.

especially from dietary aberrations. Ensure your love is not misplaced. Beware extraordinary demands on your time or generosity.

Naudiz represents need, hardship or adversity. Luckily, it includes the perseverance to endure, and reserves of inner strength. It counsels patience. However unpleasant the hardship may be, it will prove a learning experience that will ultimately benefit you. Naudiz can also warn against taking a risky path. In conjunction with other runes, Naudiz tends to have a delaying influence.

PERSONAL INTERPRETATION

You are getting exactly what you need right now to make the best progress along your spiritual path. It may appear to be the very opposite of what you want, but this state is not permanent, it is merely a series of lessons that must be learned so that you can make the transition from negative to positive. Accept your past, keep your mind fixed on your goal, and learn from your present situation. The past is just a memory, the future just a dream, the present is the only place where you have influence.

Reverse: Naudiz reversed is not obvious, so be careful. A sufficiency, something unwanted or superfluous. Have more fun with your food. Give freely of your emotions.

Converse: Your desires have hidden dangers. Demands may be misleading. Someone secretly admires you.

ASSOCIATIONS

Runic Number:	10
Colour:	Black
Gemstone:	Lapis Lazuli
Tree:	Rowan (Mountain Ash)
Herb or Plant:	Snakeroot
Element:	Fire
Polarity:	Female

Associated god: Skuld
Astrological Correspondence: Capricorn

THE RUNE POEM
Verse X Naudiz
Hardship lies heavy on the heart
Yet oft to the children of men
It becomes nonetheless a help and a
healing,
If they heed it in time.

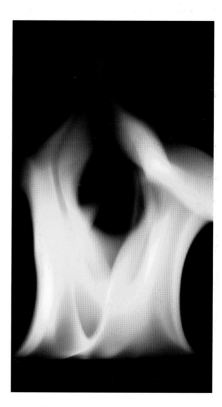

ISA

THE ICE RUNE

NAMES AND MEANINGS

Anglo-Friesian/Germanic: Isa

Norse (Viking): Is

Old English: Is

Other Names/Spellings: Eis, Icz, Isar, Isaz, Iss

Pronunciation: Ee-saw

English Letter Equivalent: I (short) as in sit

Translation: Ice

Meaning: Ice, cold, freezing. Lack of change, stagnation, lack of emotion. Storing, binding. Bridge across danger

CHARACTERISTICS

Isa means ice, and although it may be beautiful it is also dangerous. It may be slippery or treacherously thin, or it may block your progress. Isa indicates you may have to delay your plans until a more favourable season. But it can take the heat out of a confrontation, or protect against magical attack. Emotionally, Isa implies a cooling of affection or frigidity. It has a freezing, delaying, or preserving effect on other runes around it.

PERSONAL INTERPRETATION

A period of non-action is indicated. Do not let yourself get into a rut. Do not take

anyone for granted. Be not afraid to show your feelings. Crossing water will be beneficial. Things appear to be at a

The plant henbane (Hyoscyamus niger *), the alder tree, and astrologically the Moon are associated with the Isa rune. The 18th card of the Tarot's Arcana Major is also the Moon, and one of its influences is stagnation or resistance to change.*

standstill and this is not a time to try to force movement. Patience and wisdom are called for; this is not the time to

abandon goals, but an opportunity to reaffirm them. This is a time for contemplation and preparation, not for despondency or regrets. Things will change as surely as winter changes to spring and then to summer.

Reverse: Isa has no reverse.

Converse: Coolness hides emotion. An impending change will not be of benefit. Smiles mask evil intentions.

ASSOCIATIONS

Runic Number: 11
Colour: Black
Gemstone: Cat's Eye
Tree: Alder
Herb or Plant: Henbane
Element: Ice: (i.e. Water)
Polarity: Female
Associated gods: Verdandi (of the Norns)
Astrological Correspondence: The Moon

THE RUNE POEM

Verse XI Isa

Ice is extremely cold, immeasurably slippery.
It glistens clear as glass;
Most like to gems.
Is a floor wrought of frost a fair sight?

JERA

THE RUNE OF SUCCESS & CONTINUITY

NAMES AND MEANINGS

Anglo-Friesian/Germanic: Jera

Norse (Viking): Ar

Old English: Ger

Other Names/Spellings: Gaar, Jara, Jer, Jeran, Yer

Pronunciation: Year-ah

English Letter Equivalent: J as in jam. Y as in yap

Translation: Year, harvest

Meaning: Harvest, the agricultural year, fertility, fruition

CHARACTERISTICS

Success in endeavours, fruition of plans. Good spirits. Just rewards for past efforts. Inventiveness, talent or skill. Great reward is coming to those who work with their hands or on the land. Jera as the 12th rune represents the 12 months of the year. It implies fruitfulness, profit or achievement of a goal. It also means the cycle of the seasons, implying movement, change, natural development. It is usually very positive, but as a symbol of cause-and-effect it may portend the end result of past actions. Jera may therefore represent justice, which can be positive or negative, a reward or a punishment.

PERSONAL INTERPRETATION

This is a time to reap the rewards of seeds sown in the past. It is a time of plenty, of joy and celebration. But it is

*The herb rosemary (*Rosmarinus officinalis*), the oak tree, fertility and a fruitful harvest are all attributes of the rune Jera.*

also a time to work, leaving no time for complacency. The harvest is followed by winter so you should make sure you have stored enough wisdom to face your next challenge. This is another turning point in life, not a goal. There are greater harvests ahead but, like the farmer, you must prepare the land, sow the seed, tend the seedlings and nourish the fruit.

Reverse: Jera has no reverse.

Converse: Success or reward must be rooted out. You have latent talents or abilities which must be discovered.

ASSOCIATIONS

Runic Number: 12
Colour: Light Blue
Gemstone: Carnelian
Tree: Oak
Herb or Plant: Rosemary
Element: Earth
Polarity: Male and Female
Associated gods: Frey, Freya
Astrological Correspondence: The Sun

THE RUNE POEM
Verse XII Jera
Harvest is the hope of men, then the gods,
Heaven's holy Kings,
Allow the earth to yield
To prince and pauper, glorious fruits.

IHWAZ

THE RUNE OF DEFENCE

NAMES AND MEANINGS

Anglo-Friesian/Germanic: Ihwaz

Norse (Viking): Eihwaz

Old English: Eoh

Other Names/Spellings: Eihwas, Eihwaz, Eo, Erwaz, Ezck, Ihwar, Ihwas, Iwar, Iwaz, Yr

Pronunciation: Eye-warz

English Letter Equivalent: Y as in yew or long I as in side

Translation: Yew tree

Meaning: Yew tree, archer's bow, weapon. Magic, deflection, prevention

CHARACTERISTICS

Ihwaz is the symbol of rune magic. Avertive, deflective or defensive power is yours. Patience, perseverance, foresight and protection against unexpected attack. Wisdom in adversity. The yew tree has mistakenly been linked with death because of the ancient practice of planting it in graveyards, usually as hedges, when the real reason was to keep out unwanted scavenging animals; the evergreen yew is both poisonous and can present an impenetrable barrier throughout the year.

Because Ihwaz is the 13th rune, it is the origin of the 'unlucky thirteen' superstition of Anglo-Saxon culture. Ihwaz should not be feared, however, because it also means continuity and endurance.

116

The best longbows were always made from yew, making them strong, long-lasting and flexible; they were also said to contain protective magic. Thus Ihwaz also represents both safety from attack and a weapon of defence.

PERSONAL INTERPRETATION

This is a time of transformation, a time to let go of the old and embrace new beginnings, a new life and new dreams. The only constant is change, and rapid progress requires an acceptance of change rather than resistance to it. Don't be afraid: change is daunting but, if you remain true to yourself and stick to your path, you will soon achieve your goal.

Reverse: Ihwaz has no reverse.

Converse: Your defensive abilities are dormant and must be realized. What appears as a danger will be easily averted through patience and concentrated effort.

ASSOCIATIONS

Runic Number:	13
Colour:	Magenta
Gemstone:	Topaz

*The yew, the zodiac sign of Scorpio, the gemstone topaz, and the shrub lilac (*Syringa vulgaris*) are all associated with Ihwaz, the rune of defence.*

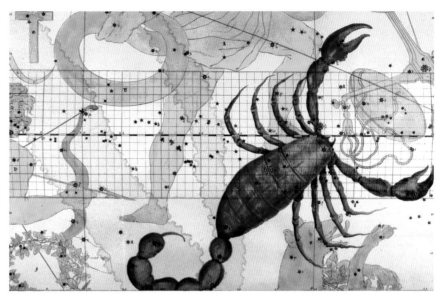

Tree:	Yew
Herb or Plant:	Lilac
Elements:	Earth, Air, Fire and Water
Polarity:	Male
Associated god:	Ullr

Astrological Correspondence: Scorpio

THE RUNE POEM

Verse XIII Ihwaz

The Yew is a rough tree without,
Fixed hard in the earth, the fire's herd,
Sustained by its roots,
A delight on the homeland.

PERTH

THE RUNE OF CHANCE, MYSTERY & SCIENCE

NAMES AND MEANINGS

Anglo-Friesian/Germanic: Perth

Norse (Viking): Pertho, Peorth

Old English: Peorth

Other Names/Spellings: Pairthra, Perb, Perthu, Peordh, Perthro, Perthrold, Pertra

Pronunciation: Pair-dth

English Letter Equivalent: P as in pot

Translation: Literal translation is not certain, but it is usually taken to be the name of a dice cup, or the name of a game of chance that might employ such a cup

Meaning: Mystery, chance, a gamble, pot luck. In modern usage, science and technology

CHARACTERISTICS

A gamble, a mystery, an unknown outcome, mathematical odds. Make the best of your lot. Use your own common

sense and sense of moderation to succeed. Spiritually, Perth suggests the disclosure of a secret, and it could also refer to pregnancy and birth. Perth is linked with the sensible and moderate enjoyment of sexuality. Because of the mystery surrounding Perth, common sense and prudence are called for in its interpretation.

PERSONAL INTERPRETATION

There is an element of choice in everything. No one can upset you, you can only choose to be upset. No one can

Reverse: Take no chances: failure is likely. What appears clear-cut hides a deeper meaning. You are tempted to be rash, but do not succumb.

Converse: A proposition has hidden depths. Take nothing for granted and only trust your loved ones.

ASSOCIATIONS

Runic Number:	14
Colour:	Black
Gemstone:	Aquamarine
Tree:	Aspen
Herb or Plant:	Aconite
Element:	Water
Polarity:	Female
Associated god:	Frigg
Astrological Correspondence:	Saturn

THE RUNE POEM

Verse XIV Perth

The Peorth is ever the play and laughter
Of proud men . . .
Where warriors sit blithely
Together in the beer-hall.

exert power over you unless you choose to subject yourself to it. Claim your right to choose, and don't allow others to compromise your truth or prevent you from doing what you need to do. The only danger here is not to make a choice at all, but to leave things to fate when you will have no say in your own future.

The aquamarine, the aspen, the aconite (monkshood or wolf's bane), the planet Saturn, and the element water all have links with the rune Perth.

ALGIZ

THE RUNE OF PROTECTION & OPPORTUNITY

NAMES AND MEANINGS

Anglo-Friesian/Germanic: Algiz

Norse (Viking): Yr

Old English: Eolh

Other names/spellings: Elhaz, Algir, Algis, Algs, Elgr

Pronunciation: Awl-gh-eeze

English Letter Equivalent: Z as in zone. S as in cousin. May also have been the rolling RRR heard in Scottish dialect

Translation: Possibly pinewoods, or more likely elk sedge, a grass-like wetland reed

Meaning: Opportunity for growth, rapid development, protection, a safe refuge

CHARACTERISTICS

Algiz illustrates both the antlers of the elk and the shape of the elk sedge plant. To some it suggests the spread fingers of a hand raised in a protective gesture. It is a powerful rune of protection and spiritually it symbolizes reaching up towards the divine.

Algiz is associated with the god Heimdall, the zodiac sign Cancer, and with the elk sedge (Carex geyeri) and pinewoods.

Algiz also represents success through endeavour in a search, quest, or other enterprise. Like the fast-growing pine tree, schemes will develop quickly. Like sharp-edged sedge, you are protected from attack. Alertness and awareness will be your guide. Wisdom, vision and clarity of mind will aid your cause.

PERSONAL INTERPRETATION

Although the path ahead is fraught with danger, you need have no fear, for the power of protection is within you, keeping you safe as long as you are not reckless.

Algiz indicates a favourable time for risky ventures, although all things must be built upon firm foundations. Do not allow yourself to become complacent.

Reverse: Slow growth or decline. You may be unprotected, be open to attack. Beware being pig-headed or short-sighted.

Converse: Growth or development opportunities are disguised. Insurance may not be as effective as you had hoped.

ASSOCIATIONS

Runic Number:	15
Colour:	Gold
Gemstone:	Amethyst
Tree:	Service Tree
Herb or Plant:	Elk Sedge
Element:	Air
Polarity:	Male
Associated god:	Heimdall
Astrological Correspondence:	Cancer

THE RUNE POEM

Verse XV Algiz
The Elk Sedge has its home most oft in the fen.
It waxes in water, wounds grimly.
The blood burns of every man
Who makes any grasp at it.

SOWILO

THE RUNE OF ENERGY & REVELATION

NAMES AND MEANINGS

Anglo-Friesian/Germanic: Sowilo

Norse (Viking): Sol, Sowulo, Sunna

Old English: Sigil, Sigel

Other Names/Spellings: Saugil, Sighel, Sigo, Sil, Sowela, Sowilu, Sowelu, Solwulo, Sugil, Sulhil, Sulu, Sygel

Pronunciation: Soh-veal-oh

English Letter Equivalent: Soft C as in nice, S as in sit

Translation: The sun

Meaning: Wholeness, light, energy, victory, discovery, disclosure

CHARACTERISTICS

The spirit of life, the energy of the sun. Completeness, spiritual awareness, boundless energy, strength of character. The capacity to learn, the gift of understanding. Good health and fitness. Although Sowilo is well-known as a victory symbol, it can also be used as a force for attack. It is a positive force, however, because it is the natural power of the sun. Spiritually, Sowilo symbolizes clear vision and the victories of light over darkness and good over evil. It warns us to use the powers of good to vanquish evil.

PERSONAL INTERPRETATION

You have the power to bring things to fruition. Good fortune awaits you and there is a positive feel to everything. This is not a time to rest and relax but to examine the darker aspects of your own nature. The power of the sun will enable you to face them without fear and to overcome them. Seek solutions to problems, they are all within your grasp.

Reverse: Sowilo has no reverse.

Converse: The eclipse of light or

Sowilo is associated with the ruby gemstone, the sun, mistletoe and the juniper tree.

energy. Hidden information, misunderstanding. Health worries are unfounded.

ASSOCIATIONS

Runic Number:	16
Colour:	White
Gemstone:	Ruby
Tree:	Juniper
Herb or Plant:	Mistletoe
Element:	Air
Polarity:	Male
Associated god:	Baldr
Astrological Correspondence:	The Sun

THE RUNE POEM

Verse XVI Sowilo

The Sun is ever the hope of seamen
When they fare over the fishes' bath,
Until the sea-steed
Brings them to land.

TIWAZ

THE WARRIOR'S RUNE

NAMES AND MEANINGS

Anglo-Friesian/Germanic: Tiwaz

Norse (Viking): Tiw, Tyr

Old English: Tir, Tyr

Other Names/Spellings: Teiws, Teiwaz, Tiwar, Ty, Tys

Pronunciation: Tee-wahz

English Letter Equivalent: T as in top

Translation: The god Tiw

Meaning: Tiw, the god of battles and legislation, the protector of warriors and mariners. Courage, compassion

CHARACTERISTICS

Tactical genius, courage, bravery, dedication, daring. Protection on sea

voyages. Negotiating and legislative ability.

Tiwaz is named for the Norse god Tiw, after whom Tuesday is also named. Tiw is the Norse equivalent of Zeus or Jupiter, and he is the god of war, justice, regulation, and success through sacrifice. He is courageous, fearless, the master tactician and a consummate diplomat. He permitted a wolf to bite off his right hand in order to bind the wolf's chaotic force. Thus he protects warriors (both physical and spiritually), the disabled and the left-handed. Tiwaz also represents determination and male sexuality. It symbolizes new challenges and initiations into new understandings.

Personal Interpretation

There is a need for courage now, as your victory is already assured if your heart remains true. Make use of all the skills and wisdom you have acquired so far. Protect your faith, as it will be challenged. But truth, honesty and justice will always win through.

Reverse: Naiveté, shyness. You must overcome a tendency towards cowardice. Loss of concentration. Beware of left-handed people.

Converse: Uncover your hidden talents of leadership. One who appears to be a fool is in fact courageous.

Associations

Runic Number:	17
Colour:	Bright Red
Gemstone:	Coral
Tree:	Oak
Herb or Plant:	Aconite
Element:	Air
Polarity:	Male
Associated god:	Tiw
Astrological Correspondence:	Libra

The Rune Poem

Verse XVII Tiwaz

Tiw is a certain sign – it keeps trust well,
With Aethlings, ever on course,
Over the night-fogs,
It never fails.

Coral, aconite, the zodiac sign Libra and the oak tree are all linked with the rune Tiwaz.

BERKANAN

THE RUNE OF GROWTH & FERTILITY

NAMES AND MEANINGS

Anglo-Friesian/Germanic: Berkanan

Norse (Viking): Bjarkan

Old English: Beorc

Other names/spellings: Bairkan, Bercna, Berkana, Berkano, Beroc

Pronunciation:Bear-khan-awn

English Letter Equivalent: B as in bag

Translation: Birch-twig

Meaning: Growth, fertility, re-birth. New life, a new broom. Physical beauty or stature

CHARACTERISTICS

Physical or mental growth. Increased business, investment or profit. Bumper

crops. Lost causes may be redeemed. New beginnings will flourish.

Berkanan refers to renewal, regeneration, purification, healing and recovery. It is the rune of the family and the home, and represents the enjoyment of sexual relations, fertility and birth. Birth in this context can be either literal or symbolic, such as the successful realization of any new idea or enterprise.

PERSONAL INTERPRETATION

An exciting time for new beginnings or fresh adventures. Activity and energy is indicated. Sow seeds, but the harvest is

yet to come, so don't expect immediate reward for your efforts. Put the past in its place, learn from experience. A good time for spiritual renewal; clear away misconceptions and accept new ideas.

Reverse: Lack of growth or reduction in stature. Decline or loss of business, profits or crops. A bad time for new ventures.

Converse: Increased size or profit is being hidden or dishonestly withheld. You may suffer a theft. An investment that looks risky may well be safe.

The zodiac sign of Virgo, the birch tree, the moonstone and lady's mantle (Alchemilla) are linked with Berkanan.

ASSOCIATIONS

Runic Number: 18

Colour: Dark Green

Gemstone: Moonstone

Tree: Birch

Herb or Plant: Lady's Mantle

Element: Earth

Polarity: Female

Associated god: Nerthus (Mother Holda)

Astrological Correspondence: Virgo

THE RUNE POEM

Verse XVIII Berkanan

The Birch is fruitless, nonetheless it bears
Shoots without seed; it is beauteous in
 boughs
High of helm, fairly adorned
Laden with leaves, close to the sky.

EHWAZ

THE RUNE OF MOMENTUM

NAMES AND MEANINGS

Anglo-Friesian/Germanic: Ehwaz

Norse (Viking): Eoh

Old English: Eh, Oe or Eoh

Other Names/Spellings: Aihws, Ehol, Ehwar, Eol, Eow, Eykur, Eys, Ior

Pronunciation: Ay-wahz

English Letter Equivalent: E as in end, EE as in sheet

Translation: Horse, steed

Meaning: Horse, beast of burden, steed or mount. Momentum, speed

CHARACTERISTICS

Speed of thought or deed, quick-wittedness. Forward progress, purposeful

motion. Willingness. Surefooted, confident, loyal.

Ehwaz represents the horse, whose speed, strength and beauty makes it much more than a means of transport. It is a sacred animal, a vehicle for material and spiritual advancement. Ehwaz implies controlled change, progress, and sometimes a journey. It also represents partnership, trust, loyalty and faithfulness, such as that which exists between horse and rider, brother and sister, two halves of the whole.

PERSONAL INTERPRETATION

You have the support you need to make swift progress towards your goal. But you must be loyal and supportive to those around you, as they are to you. The horse is proud, but that does not impede its purpose. So while you may be proud of your achievements you must remain

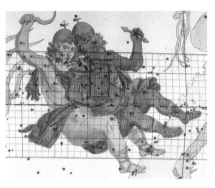

humble to ensure your journey reaches a successful conclusion.

Reverse: Lethargy, retrograde motion, regression. Muddled thinking.

Reluctance, diffidence. Becoming lost or bemused.

Converse: That which appears stagnant will suddenly flow. Someone seemingly willing or confident will be up to no good.

ASSOCIATIONS

Runic Number:	19
Colour:	White
Gemstone:	Iceland Spar
Tree:	Ash
Herb or Plant:	Ragwort
Element:	Earth
Polarity:	Male and Female
Associated gods:	Frey, Freya
Astrological Correspondence: Gemini	

The Rune Poem
Verse XIX Ehwaz
A Steed is the joy of aethlings or eorls,
A horse proud of hoof, where men
about It,
Wealthy, on stallions, swap speech,
And to the unquiet is ever a solace.

*The ragwort (*Senecio*), a plant poisonous to horses, the Iceland spar, the ash tree, the zodiac sign of Gemini, the Twins, and the horse itself, are all associated with Ehwaz.*

MANNAZ

THE RUNE OF HUMANITY

NAMES AND MEANINGS

Anglo-Friesian/Germanic: Mannaz

Norse (Viking): Madr

Old English: Man

Other Names/Spellings: Madhr, Madthr, Madthur, Mann, Manna, Mannar, Mannazold

Pronunciation: Mah-nawz

English Letter Equivalent: M as in man

Translation: Mankind, human

Meaning: Mankind, humanity. The self, the inner being, the soul. Manhood or womanhood

CHARACTERISTICS

Yourself, your mind and ego, your body. People in general, the world, friends or family or associates. Clarity of thought.

Tolerance, broad-mindedness. Devotion, kindness, consideration and charity. Willing to change.

Mannaz represents the human race, humanity, the shared human nature within each individual. We are all members of the human family, yet are alone in life and in the final journey into death. Mannaz symbolizes creativity, intelligence, forward-planning, and speech, and implies cooperation between individuals for the common good.

PERSONAL INTERPRETATION

Destiny awaits you, so claim it. But to be a spiritual being, you must balance body, mind and spirit. Embrace everything, good and bad alike, with total acceptance, knowing that each new experience will teach more of life. By learning each lesson you will go onwards and upwards.

Reverse: Refers the same portents to a person of the opposite sex to yourself,

e.g. a husband, wife, partner, mother, father etc.

Converse: The person referred to is being covert or dishonest.

ASSOCIATIONS

Runic Number: 20
Colour: Deep Red
Gemstone: Garnet
Tree: Holly
Herb or Plant: Madder
Element: Air
Polarity: Male and Female
Associated gods: Heimdall, Odin, Frigg
Astrological Correspondence: Jupiter

THE RUNE POEM
Verse XX Mannaz
A mirthful Man is to his kinsmen dear;
Yet each one must from the others turn,
Because Odin desires by his decree
To deliver that frail flesh to earth.

The garnet gemstone, the god Odin, the planet Jupiter, and the holly, are some of Mannaz's correspondences.

RIGHT: Jupiter and Sémélé, 1895, by Gustave Moreau.

145

LAGUZ

THE WATER RUNE

NAMES AND MEANINGS

Anglo-Friesian/Germanic: Laguz

Norse (Viking): Logr, Laukaz

Old English: Lagu

Other Names/Spellings: Laaz, Lagur, Lagus, Laukar, Laukr, Logur

Pronunciation: Lah-gooze

English Letter Equivalent: L as in let

Translation: Water, lake, lagoon

Meaning: Water, sea, ocean, river or lake. Cleansing, the tide

CHARACTERISTICS

Associations with water in all its forms. Cleansing action. Tidal movement: ebb

and flow. Fortuitous omen for overseas travel, fishing or other aquatic activities.

Laguz means water, a vital part of life but a constant danger, just as our journey through life involves risks. Laguz contains elements of fluidity, changeability, and a lack of control. It represents the sensual madness of sexuality, the unconscious, intuitive and psychic abilities. Its deceptive elements come from its variety rather than from any menace. Traditionally, Laguz is the ultimate female rune.

PERSONAL INTERPRETATION

Only by attuning yourself with creation will your life truly flow as it is ordained. I use 'creation' here for want of a better word: what I mean is everything you perceive, both physically and spiritually.

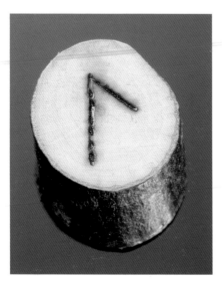

This includes the natural world, the Earth, its land and oceans, its flora and fauna; and it includes the world of people, with all the nations and cultures encompassed within it. But it also includes all things spiritual that may impinge on your mind and your soul, whether they arise from within or from contact with the domain of the gods and spirits.

Emotional balance comes from being in harmony with creation around you: for example, natural foods lead to a natural flow, whereas unnatural foods lead to disharmony and stagnation. The sea is

always fluid and moving, so it should be with your life. Embrace change for its own sake, for it is the only true constant in life.

Reverse: Storm, flood, waves, corrosion or other destructive action of water. Danger of sinking or drowning.

Converse: Beware mariners or others associated with water, who may be trying to trick you.

ASSOCIATIONS
Runic Number: 21
Colour: Dark Green
Gemstone: Pearl
Tree: Osier Willow
Herb or Plant: Leek
Element: Water

Polarity: Female
Associated gods: Njord, Nerthus
Astrological Correspondence: The Moon

THE RUNE POEM
Verse XXI Laguz
Water seems interminable to men
If they should venture on a shaky bark;
And the sea-surges greatly frighten them,
And the sea-steed takes no heed of the
curb.

The pearl, the leek, the osier willow, the god Njord, water and lagoons, are some of Laguz's correspondences.

INGWAZ

THE RUNE OF PEACE & HARMONY

NAMES AND MEANINGS

Anglo-Friesian/Germanic: Ingwaz

Norse (Viking): Inguz

Old English: Ing

Other Names/Spellings: Enguz, Iggus, Ingvarr, Ingwar

Pronunciation: Ing-wahz

English Letter Equivalent: NG diphthong, as in finger

Translation: An angel. The god Ing

Meaning: Harmony, approval, unity, agreement, love, peace

CHARACTERISTICS

Ingwaz is named for the Norse hero-god Ing, who came from across the sea to

unite his people of Viking Jutland, and returned whence he came leaving peace and harmony. Ingwaz representing Ing therefore symbolizes peace, unity, harmony, agreement, togetherness and undying love between romantic partners.

It portends completion, the certainty of a conclusion. This could include the male orgasmic force, or birth as the conclusion to a pregnancy. Ingwaz is associated with healthy, wholesome sexuality, a strong, affectionate family, and a safe, secure hearth and home. It also symbolizes protection, and exemplifies the idea of a beacon, a light shining in the darkness, and therefore spiritual inspiration.

PERSONAL INTERPRETATION

On your spiritual path you may feel isolated, but within you burns the fire of inspiration, urging you onward and upward. Feed the fire by perseverance. Seek answers but don't allow yourself to become encumbered by irrelevant questions. Live one day at a time, knowing that the past is a memory and the future a mere dream; remember that the here and now is what really matters.

Reverse: Ingwaz has no reverse.

Converse: Love, harmony or peace may be hard to achieve, but persevere. A lover may be shy – help them to declare themselves.

ASSOCIATIONS

Runic Number: 22
Colour: Yellow
Gemstone: Amber
Tree: Apple
Herb or Plant: Selfheal
Element: Earth and Water
Polarity: Male
Associated gods: Ing, Frey
Astrological Correspondence: Cancer, the New Moon

THE RUNE POEM

Verse XXII Ingwaz

Ing was amongst the East-Danes first
*   seen by men,*
Till later east he went over the wave;
His wain followed after;
The Heardings named the hero so.

The rune Ingwaz is associated with amber,
the Norse god Frey, romantic love, and the
apple tree, among other attributes.

OTHILA

THE RUNE OF FAMILY, HOME & ACQUISITION

NAMES AND MEANINGS

Anglo-Friesian/Germanic: Othila

Norse (Viking): Odal

Old English: Odal, Ethel

Other Names/Spellings: Odhal, Odthal, Ogthala, Otael, Othal, Othala, Othalan, Othilia, Utal

Pronunciation: Oh-thee-law

English Letter Equivalent: Long O as in old, or short O as in cot

Translation: Hereditary land, possession

Meaning: Home or homeland, hearth and home, family, inheritance, estate, possessions

CHARACTERISTICS

Acquisition: benefit through inheritance or birthright. Fair play. Great mental capacity. An adventurous nature. Cultural maturity. Personal skill, adaptability. Love of family, home and homeland, patriotism. The honest and just are destined for great wealth.

Othila means the ancestral country or home, property and fixed wealth or inheritance. This can include characteristics you have inherited from past generations that you will also pass on to your children, or it can represent a

united family's strength. Othila can be seen as everything you may have accumulated during your lifetime, and can also represent your spiritual home.

PERSONAL INTERPRETATION

At this time of refocusing, fix your goal firmly in your mind and let your thoughts attract the energy you need to achieve it. You must concentrate and read all the signs, but don't try to force the issue. Your objective is like a wild bird in the palm of your hand: grip it too tightly and you risk killing it.

Reverse: A valueless inheritance. Lack of forethought. Immaturity or dullness. Failure to take a calculated risk would be costly.

Converse: An apparently worthless inheritance conceals hidden treasures. The honest or just way may be hidden from you.

ASSOCIATIONS

Runic Number:	23
Colour:	Deep Yellow
Gemstone:	Spinel
Tree:	Hawthorn
Herb or Plant:	White Clover
Element:	Earth
Polarity:	Male
Associated gods:	Odin
Astrological Correspondence: Full Moon	

THE RUNE POEM

Verse XXIII Othila

An Estate is greatly dear to every man
If what is right and fitting there
He may enjoy at home
With most prosperity.

*The rune Othila is linked with the hawthorn, white clover (*Trifolium repens*), and the full moon.*

DAGAZ

THE RUNE OF TRANSFORMATION,

NAMES AND MEANINGS

Anglo-Friesian/Germanic: Dagaz

Norse (Viking): Dag, Daeg

Old English: Daeg

Other names/spellings: Daaz, Dagr, Dagar, Dagur, Dags, Daguz

Pronunciation: Daw-ghawz

English Letter Equivalent: D as in dog, DJ as in Django Reinhardt, DTH as in breadth

Translation: Day

Meaning: Day, daylight, dawn Breakthrough. Radical change

CHARACTERISTICS

A breakthrough, a new dawn or a major change of direction. Achievement and prosperity, a successful conclusion to a journey. Darkness is behind you because a new day has begun. Dagaz means day, and in the Nordic lands of long nights and winters, it has become strongly associated with light and life.

Dagaz is the essence of natural daylight, the new light of dawn, and the strength of the sun. Spiritually, it is the divine light, the high point of the natural cycle of darkness-light-darkness. It signifies brightness, growth, progress, development, and sometimes fundamental change.

PERSONAL INTERPRETATION

The divine light is guiding you towards your goal. Remain true, and good fortune will be with you. You are well-protected by the power of the light. It will give you clear vision to avoid dangers, but don't be blinded by your own ego. Remain humble and thankful for all the good things that have come to you.

*The clary sage (*Salvia sclarea*), the Norse god Heimdall, the waxing or waning moon, and the spruce tree, are linked with the rune Dagaz.*

Reverse: Dagaz has no reverse.

Converse: A false dawn; the time is not right for change and the daylight is yet to come. Persevere and trust in your own strength and ability.

ASSOCIATIONS

Runic Number:	24
Colour:	Light Blue
Gemstone:	Chrysolite
Tree:	Spruce
Herb or Plant:	Clary Sage

Element:	Fire and Air
Polarity:	Male
Associated gods:	Heimdall

Astrological Correspondence: Waxing or Waning Moon

THE RUNE POEM

Verse XXIV Dagaz

Day is Odin's messenger, dear to men,
The Ruler's glorious light,
Mirth and hope to prosperous and poor,
Useful to all.

THE BLANK

NAMES AND MEANINGS

Anglo-Saxon: Woden, Voden, Vodan

Norse: Odin, Ohdinn

Old English: Woden, Weden, Wotan

Translation: The blank is a concept of modern origin and has no traditional value or significance. Because it is blank, it can hardly be considered a rune at all

Meaning: Fate or destiny. The will of the gods. The end or the beginning, death or birth. The appearance of the blank would, I suppose, signify that in this aspect, fate has taken control and left you with none. The death or birth indications should be taken as symbolic rather than actual and would, I imagine, refer to any aspect of

your life, such as work, romance, business or wealth.

CHARACTERISTICS

The invention of the blank is usually ascribed to Ralph Blum, the author of the 1980s, *The Book of Runes*, a very personal view of runic divination much criticized for its inaccuracies. But it is probable that the concept of a blank was formulated during the Renaissance, possibly as early as the 16th century. I have no documentary evidence to support this claim, only vague suggestions that I have garnered here and there.

I do not use the blank myself, preferring the traditional method, but it is included here for those interested in using it. It is often taken to represent fate, destiny or Odin, the high god of Scandinavian tradition and of runic

magic, the god of creation, victory and the dead.

Traditionally, Ansuz is Odin's rune, so I can't really see the need for another piece to represent him, especially a blank. However, the associations given here are applicable to Odin, so for those who want them, I have arbitrarily ascribed them to the blank. Those who use the blank in divination will no doubt grow to recognize that it is superfluous as they progress in runic knowledge. Moreover, the use of the blank in divination is a matter provoking much controversy and discussion in books and websites concerned with the runes and their attributes.

PERSONAL INTERPRETATION

Must be based on the adjacent runes in the cast.

The blank rune has no reverse or converse.

ASSOCIATIONS

A blank would obviously have no real associations, so these are the ones applicable to Odin.

The blank rune, having none of its own, has been given Odin's attributes, including the tourmaline, the ash tree and the marigold.

Runic Number: Since the blank is not a rune, zero would be the obvious choice.

Colour: Runic Blue

Gemstone: Tourmaline

Tree: Ash

Herb or Plant: Marigold (*Calendula*)

Element: Air

Polarity: Male

Associated gods: Odin

Astrological Correspondence: Mercury

THE RUNE POEM

As explained above, the blank is not really a rune at all, so it is not therefore featured in the Rune Poem. The verses given in the other pages are from a transcription of the Anglo-Saxon Rune Poem.

A note about the verses from the Rune Poem, that appear throughout Chapter 3:

The original Rune Poem manuscript was kept in the Cotton Library at Oxford University. Many students were in the habit of copying documents for their own use and luckily the Anglo-Saxon scholar, Humfrey Wanley, made a copy of the Rune Poem to prepare a transcription of his own. This transcript was included in a thesaurus by Dr. George Hickes, entitled *Linguarum Veterum Septentrionalium Thesaurus Grammatico: Criticus et Archaeologicus*, published in 1703. In 1731 the Cotton Library was seriously damaged by fire and the original Rune Poem manuscript was destroyed.

No one is quite sure how accurate the Wanley/Hickes transcription is, but it is the only document on the subject with any provenance that still exists. The verses given in this chapter are from a translation into modern English by the Anglo-Saxon scholar, Dr. Louis J. Rodrigues, while writing his doctoral thesis at Cambridge University. His book, *Anglo-Saxon Verse Runes*, is listed in the bibliography at the end of this book.

165

DOWSING WITH THE
RUNIC PENDULUM

CHAPTER FOUR
DOWSING WITH THE RUNIC PENDULUM

INTRODUCTION

As an alternative to divining with the runes, you might like to consider the lesser-known art of dowsing with a pendulum. My friend, Mark Porter, and I, developed a runic version of the dowsing pendulum and found it to be quite effective for certain types of enquiry.

The pendulum is a good tool for divination where you are seeking simple answers to direct, uncomplicated questions. The runic pendulums supplied on my website have been empowered with eight runes, to enhance the instruments' power both to 'send' and 'receive'.

SEND RUNES

1 Ansuz

2 Ingwaz

3 Ihwaz

4 Ehwaz

A typical runic pendulum: when using this, both mind and body should be as calm and relaxed as possible.

RECEIVE RUNES

1 Raido

2 Berkanan

3 Dagaz

4 Sowilo

Should you decide to make your own instrument, you can empower it yourself by adapting the ritual for Bindrunes on page 188 of Chapter 5.

THE DOWSING SYSTEM

Dowsing is a spiritual matter in which the conscious and the intuitive areas of the brain, sometimes called the subconscious, are joined. In the dowsing process, the pendulum becomes the focus on which one can concentrate to bring unperceived knowledge to the awareness of the conscious mind. Therefore, by practising with the runic pendulum, points of contact can be created between the conscious and subconscious minds.

Using the pendulum protects you from losing your way or indeed becoming anxious about making contact with the spiritual ether. When you feel comfortable and confident enough with the method you will be able to explore all kinds of situations without fear of stumbling into threatening situations.

There are a number of traditional ways of using a pendulum, but don't let anyone tell you how to do it; there are no rules to follow, and everyone should develop their own procedure to discover a system that works for them. The system comprises the pendulum, the body, the conscious mind, and the subconscious or inner self which is often called the spirit or soul.

Mastering the process is like learning any skill. You experiment with

techniques, you practise with materials, and you familiarize yourself with tools or equipment. If you were learning to paint you would discover, over time, your own preferences for brushes, types of paint, surfaces on which to work and so on. You would develop your own style based on those preferences and your own personal strengths and weaknesses.

In the same way it is your own decision how you use the pendulum, and you must find the way that produces the best results for you, rather than follow rules laid down by others. If you already have a procedure that works for you, continue to use it, but if you are new to subject, or have had little success so far, try these preparatory exercises first.

SETTING THE SYSTEM UP

Your state of mind is the most important aspect of the preparation for a dowsing session. You should be calm, relaxed and free from tension. You should be concentrating on your inner thoughts and emotions and not on the pendulum itself. Some dowsers call this meditative condition the 'alpha state'.

Now consider your environment. The requirements are just the same as you would choose for a divining session with the runes. You need a quiet spot, not too brightly lit, and away from any active electrical equipment, such as a switched-on TV or washing machine. Sit in an ordinary upright chair and make yourself comfortable with your back straight and your feet on the ground, maybe about 2 or 3ft (60 or 90cm) apart.

Hold the chain of the pendulum between thumb and forefinger with your fingers pointing downwards. Start with about 3 or 4in (8 or 10cm) of chain between your fingers and the top of the

pendulum. Wrap any spare chain around your hand so that it doesn't get in the way. After you have gone through the following calibration procedures, you may like to experiment with different lengths of chain to discover what works best for you.

CALIBRATING THE SYSTEM

Calibration of the system is the next step, which is a rather grand term for discovering how you and your pendulum are likely to work together, and means setting and learning the responses to the questions you will be asking. You need to establish what the dowsing system is saying to you as represented by the movement of the pendulum.

The 'on-line' position is achieved by setting the pendulum into a to and fro swing or oscillation, towards and away from your body, midway between your knees. The swing doesn't have to be fast or very wide, a few inches will do.

Now to find out what the pendulum will do to indicate a 'yes' or a 'no' response. Keep the on-line swing going, hold the pendulum over the knee on the dominant side of your body (generally the right side for right-handed people, and left for the left-handed). As you do this, ask out loud for a yes response. You might have to repeat the request a couple of times before you notice any difference in the movement. This might be any kind of change in the swing, or sometimes the pendulum might even begin elliptically to rotate. Quite often the yes response is a clockwise swing, but that isn't always the case. Repeat this exercise a few times to

make sure you are getting the same response every time.

When you are satisfied that the yes response has been clearly established, move the swinging pendulum back to the on-line position and wait for it to settle down into the backward and forward swing. Now we are looking for the 'no' response. Move the pendulum over your non-dominant knee and ask for a no in the same way as before. Again this may be any change in the movement of the pendulum, but it most often turns out to be an anticlockwise rotation. But whatever you get has to be opposite to or a totally different reaction to the yes response.

If you find you are getting accurate responses right away, you are obviously a natural dowser and should be thankful for being so lucky. If you found that no signals emerged on their own and that the pendulum remains in its on-line state when held over either knee, try different lengths of chain or slightly different sitting positions. Make sure your mind is on the matter in hand, that you are concentrating on your own thoughts, and that you are not unconsciously trying to manipulate the pendulum.

If you are still unsuccessful, it may be that you have been distracted by something, which could be a recurring thought in your mind that just won't go away, or maybe it's something to do with your physical environment, such as outside noise, too much light or extraneous movement, or being too hot or too cold.

Another common cause is that you may be allowing yourself to become too anxious about the pendulum's failure to cooperate. Whatever the cause, you might like to consider abandoning the session until a more auspicious time. But you are quite free to simply choose your yes and no responses and force them onto the system by making your pendulum swing in the way you choose, while it is being held over the appropriate knee. This is not a fraudulent manoeuvre, you are merely establishing the responses that will be used for future communications; with repetition and practice it will become standard procedure and serve you well henceforth. If you do have to choose and programme the responses, try to induce a clockwise circle for yes and an anticlockwise one for no, which are the ones that work best for many experienced dowsers.

UNCERTAIN RESPONSES

When you have a little more experience under your belt you might like to try and develop responses for what I call 'er-um' answers, i.e. weak or hesitant responses for either yes or no, which is not the same as 'don't know' or 'can't be bothered'; you will get responses like these when you ask something that is beyond the capability of the dowsing system, or when you have become fed up with the session yourself. You will probably get nothing more than the off-line backwards and forwards swing, or perhaps even an almost stationary pendulum. But the er-um response I am recommending you to try and establish will mean 'well, yes but . . .' or 'maybe no, but . . .', and will indicate that the question was ambiguous or open to misinterpretation.

To establish these responses, think of a question that can't be answered with a straight yes or no, such as 'how old am I?', or 'what colour is grass?' You will probably get an angled to and fro swing rather that a circular motion, angled left to right meaning yes and angled right to left meaning no. They could be the other way round, of course, as could yes and no as explained above. Once again, if the pendulum doesn't seem to want to cooperate you may induce the movement by consciously moving your hand, and eventually the responses will become incorporated into your dowsing method.

When you think you have the er-um answers fixed into the system, try rephrasing the previous types of questions, for example, 'Am I 106 years old?', to which I hope you don't get a yes response! Or you might ask, 'Is the grass orange?', to which you wouldn't want a yes response either!

Practice and patience is the key to developing a working and reliable system. Bear in mind that this is a new area of knowledge for you, a new skill in which you are training your mind and body. It's not difficult mentally, or physically demanding, but it does require some effort and dedication to get it right. I would recommend you spend 10 or 15 minutes on the system every day for a few weeks. Run through the sequence of online, yes, no, er-um yes and er-um no, until the replies become automatic and instantly recognizable.

POSING QUESTIONS

Now we turn to the matter of asking questions of the system. When you first open a session, or if you are changing the subject, it would be a good idea to check that the system is going to be happy working on the question. The sort of things that are appropriate are matters under your own control, or things you think might already be hiding in your subconscious.

Appropriate questions to ask will be about things that are within your control, or about things to which your subconscious most likely already knows the answers. Good subjects for exploration are: making a choice, the best way to deal with a situation, understanding your own emotions about something, asking about someone else and their motives for doing something, asking about the emotional or physical symptoms you are experiencing, making decisions about food or dietary matters.

You may need to start with wide-ranging questions before concentrating on a specific matter. If you get fuzzy answers, think about your sequence of questions and ask yourself if you have been communicating clearly, phrasing your questions accurately and without ambiguity, or maybe you have simply been too general and need to narrow the question down some more.

A GOOD PROGRAMME FOR A NEW SESSION WOULD BE TO:

Set up the system and get the pendulum into the off-line position.

Think carefully about your questions and speak them clearly.

Ask the system if the subject matter is something you can deal with.

Ask the system if you are allowed to deal with the subject. For example, if you are dowsing for another person, you need to ask them if the subject is open to discussion before proceeding.

And finally ask if this is a good time to deal with the matter and whether or not you will be ready for the sort of answers that may be presented.

The dowsing system never works very well when idle or frivolous questions are asked. You are much more likely to get positive results and accurate answers when you are dealing with something important and of genuine interest. If you are aware that you are simply playing around, then the system and the pendulum will respond – or fail to respond – accordingly, which is your subconscious mind's way of saying 'get lost!' But if you get firm answers to all these questions then you know you are free to proceed with the session.

Communication with your subconscious, and through it the spiritual ether, is thought to behave like an energy wave form, which I believe probably vacillates between strong and weak conditions depending on your physical and mental state. Being in a state of gloom is likely to induce a weak or low point in the system and it will not be

responding very well, whereas if you are in an energetic mood, and feel ready for anything, you can expect rapid and accurate answers to good questions.

Now let's look at the way questions should be asked. The way each question is constructed is critical, as we have already seen when discussing accuracy and ambiguity. Remember that unlike questions asked of other people in conversation, you are always looking for yes or no responses. When you get poor responses that are hard to interpret you should look back on the session and see whether it was your input that caused the poor output. The old computer adage of GIGO (garbage in, garbage out) is just as true of your dowsing system.

Once the question has been asked you can expect a short delay before the pendulum begins to answer. Try to make no prejudgements of the answer: in other words, don't try to will the system to say yes or no, but concentrate on the pendulum and wait for the response without trying to guess what it will be. A good way to avoid this pitfall is to repeat the question every so often until the response appears. If you are still experiencing difficulty you might try returning to childhood. Remember how it was, wondering what you were going to

get for a birthday present? That is the state of mind that may well produce a positive response.

You can check accuracy by dowsing questions that will soon be answered. For example, when making a phone call you could first dowse to see if the person you are calling is at home, at work, or whether you will get their voicemail. But make sure that inaccuracies are not due to ambiguity in the question. If you find your dowsing unproductive, try again later when you are in a better frame of mind.

In Conclusion

Finally, if I may repeat the most critical aspect of dowsing with the pendulum: a genuine desire to unravel important issues is the best formula for accurate dowsing. It will help to direct your dowsing to important issues and align your spiritual energy with the world at large.

It can be beneficial to say 'thank you' to the system when bringing a dowsing session to a close. This will serve to keep your energy in tune with the spiritual world, satisfy your subconscious mind, and demonstrate your respect for the amazing talent you have been able to develop.

A runic pendulum made from solid hawthorn (Crataegus monogyna).

BINDRUNES

CHAPTER FIVE
BINDRUNES

INTRODUCTION

Bindrunes fall into two categories: personal bindrunes and practical bindrunes.

Personal bindrunes are the designs often used as amulets or for tattoos, where the bindrune is composed of one's personal initials to form a kind of runic monogram. They are used to reinforce one's personality and emphasize the

positive qualities of the psyche. The illustration left shows a bindrune that includes Kauno, Jera and Tiwaz to represent the initials CJT.

Practical bindrunes are used as talismans with a particular objective in

FAR LEFT: Kauno, Jera and Tiwaz combine in a bindrune to form the initials CJT.

ABOVE: Gibu Auja, the good luck bindrune, used as a tattoo.

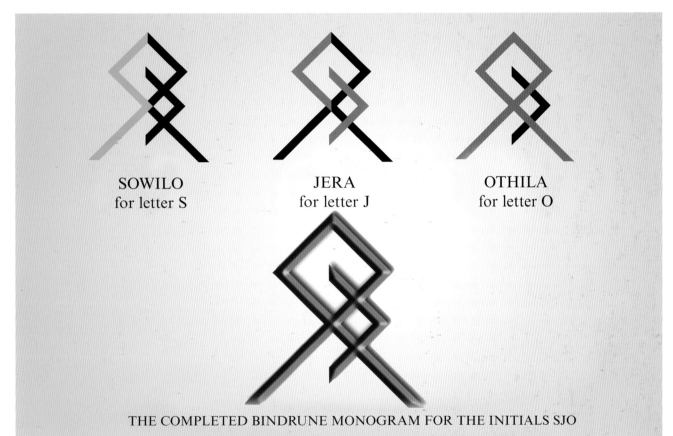

SOWILO
for letter S

JERA
for letter J

OTHILA
for letter O

THE COMPLETED BINDRUNE MONOGRAM FOR THE INITIALS SJO

mind, such as to achieve improved health, business or financial success, harmony with a partner, love from a special person, help with weight loss, personal protection, safety and security of your home and personal possessions, etc. The example shown tattooed on the wrist (opposite right) is a very ancient design that is always popular, and it says Gibu Auja, meaning 'provide good luck'.

DESIGNING PERSONAL BINDRUNES
I have designed many bindrunes for people based on their initials, in which I take the rune equivalents for the letters required and arrange them in the most attractive way possible. Sometimes the rune symbols are mirror-imaged for symmetry, and sometimes I combine two or more runes on a single stave (i.e. the perpendicular stroke).

The above illustration shows how the runes Sowilo for letter S, Jera for letter J and Othila for letter O have been combined into a bindrune monogram to represent the initials SJO. The positioning of the individual runes is highlighted in the three smaller images, the larger one being the completed bindrune.

There are many examples of ancient bindrunes designed in just such a way, so it is perfectly in keeping with runic tradition. In fact, the ancients were fairly arbitrary when it came to runes, writing them left-to-right, right-to-left, as mirror images, and sometimes even as whole sentences that appear upside-down. But as a rule I do not reverse runes (i.e. draw them upside-down), for by doing this it is generally accepted that it reverses the runes' meaning.

CONSTRUCTING A PERSONAL BINDRUNE

Runes are phonetic, in that they represent sounds rather than letters. So Kauno is the equivalent of K, in the English alphabet, as it appears in the word 'king', or a hard C as in the word 'cat'. So if your name is Colin or Catherine, your first runic initial would be Kauno, the rune that corresponds with K. But if your name is Cyril or Cecilia then you would choose S represented by Sowilo, because it is the rune that makes the soft C sound.

Names like Thora and Theodore, and others beginning with the TH sound, can be rather confusing, too. In English you would say your first initial was T, but in runes it is Thurisaz, because it is the rune that represents the TH sound all on its own. Thomas also begins with TH, but since it is normally spoken as Tomas, then Tiwaz is the correct rune to use.

The ancients did not distinguish between W and V, but used the same soft V sound for both, so that both V and W initials are represented by Wunjo.

J and Y are the most difficult letters to represent in runes; strictly speaking, the J in John or Joanne should be represented by Dagaz, because the ancients pronounced Dagaz like a DG or DZ diphthong. But in modern usage it is common to represent J as Jera, even though its real sound is like the Y in the word 'year'. There is another rune that makes the Y sound and that is Ihwaz, in that it sounds like the Y in 'young'.

There are no rune equivalents for X or Q as the ancients did not use these sounds. I usually make X using Kauno and Sowilo together to make a 'ks' sound, and Q as Kauno and Wunjo to make a 'kw' sound.

Names of German or Scandinavian origin that begin with ING are represented by Ingwaz, Inge and Ingomar being good examples. But don't be misled into using Isa because it represents the letter I – Ingwaz is much more attractive!

I usually follow these rules when compiling bindrunes for people:

K and hard C are represented by Kauno
S and soft C are represented by Sowilo.
T is represented by Tiwaz
TH is represented by Thurisaz
V and W are both represented by Wunjo
J as in John is represented by Jera
J as in Juan is represented by Hagalaz
J as in Jorge and Y as in Yolanda are represented by Ihwaz

There is a table of all the English letter equivalents on page 225 of Chapter 7.

PRACTICAL BINDRUNES

A practical bindrune may combine two or more runes to form a single design representing the runic powers of the included runes. The purpose of the bindrune is to allow a controlled release of these runic energies for the benefit of the user, or someone he or she wishes to help or influence.

Bindrunes can only be used to help people, not to harm them. Any attempt to place a curse, prevent a person from doing something, or to make something nasty happen to them, will inevitably backfire on the user. So believe me when I tell you never to attempt this.

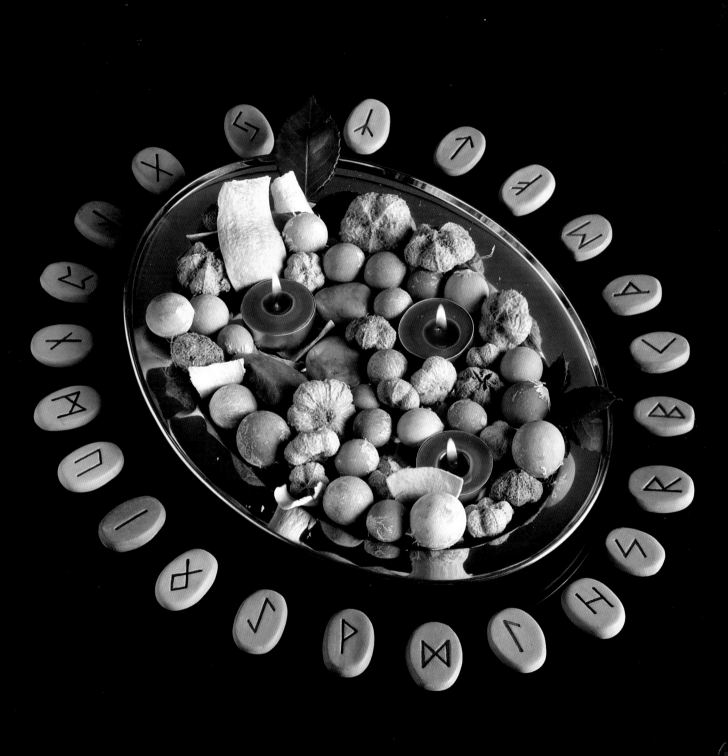

This is a practical bindrune to ensure personal protection, but another may be devised to offer a person extra speed or endurance in a competition.

Although a bindrune is a blending of runic characters, each rune included in the design has to retain its own individuality, in that it must be visible as an entity within the whole. I find it is best to limit the design to no more than four or five characters, so that it retains its symmetry, being balanced and pleasing to the eye.

There are exceptions to this rule, however. Some very ancient and highly effective bindrunes incorporate 6, 7 or even 8 different runes. But generally speaking, the simpler the design the more effective the bindrune will be.

Practical bindrunes are devised for specific purposes: they can generate mental activity, such as memory, logic, emotion, enlightenment, strength of will, courage, fairness, clarity of thought. They can enhance physical attributes too, such as health, strength, speed, endurance, as well as sharpening the five senses.

Bindrunes can also produce a runic field of energy to protect your person, your home or possessions, your job or your business, and they can improve relationships by encouraging harmony, love or sexual attraction.

It is a simple matter to draw a bindrune on a piece of paper, wood, stone, etc., carrying it with you in the hope that it will have some effect. But it would be so weak that you would be unlikely to notice any difference. For a bindrune to work effectively it must be empowered (some rune-users refer to this process as consecration) in the correct way. The exact detail of how I prepare and empower a bindrune has been a closely guarded secret for many years, but I am now revealing the entire process for the first time.

The choice of wood is of importance to the effectiveness of the bindrune. I keep about 20 types of wood so that I can always make an amulet that is compatible with its component runes.

During the whole process of cutting, polishing and branding the design, I follow an ancient ritual for naming and empowering the individual runes. This involves a special environment, chanted invocations in the old tongue, and the use of certain natural accessories.

When the bindrune is complete it is then sequestered in a sacred place for a specific period under special conditions. The place I use is a ley cross – a point where there is potent earth energy, where two positive ley lines cross one another – but any consecrated area will suffice.

For the sequesterment, the bindrune must be preserved in a particular way and hidden according to ancient rules for a set length of time that is determined by the component runes and the purpose of the bindrune itself. Then, once the bindrune has been released from sequesterment, the imbued power is awakened and invoked on behalf of the user.

AN EMPOWERMENT RITE FOR BINDRUNES
The bindrune amulets I make are empowered at the time of their creation by a rite that includes all of the actions described here, plus some additional clauses identifying the new owner of the product and some stipulations about the transfer of ownership from myself, the maker, to the customer, the new owner. It is not necessary for buyers to carry out their own form of ritual, but it will certainly do no harm if they wish to do so.

Designs, on the other hand, cannot be empowered until they have been given a physical existence on a material substance, either by carving, tattooing, or painting.

It is best to empower runic designs at the time of their creation, but this is not often practical in a tattoo studio, for example, and may be embarrassing if the artist is not a rune initiate himself. But it is possible to perform the post-creation rite at home, in private, if you prefer; this will mean tracing the design with a wet finger as if it were being created at that moment in time which, in the case of a tattoo, may be a painful thing to do in that it is as yet unhealed.

To empower any bindrune, whether it be a solid object, such as an amulet, or a design tattooed upon your own person, several items of equipment are required:

• You will need a half-pint or so of natural fresh water from a spring, river, lake or pond (not tap water). If you do not have access to a source of natural water, distilled water from the drug store or the water used for battery top-ups is good, while bottled mineral water is not.
• A candle: it doesn't matter what type, it's the heat produced that matters. But don't use a black one, which I have found to be not very effective.
• Incense: again it doesn't matter what kind – it's the smoke that counts.
• A natural fibre cloth (e.g. cotton, linen, wool), long enough to wind nine times

around the bindrune or the part of the body where the bindrune has been tattooed. If you need to use several pieces to get the nine turns, then that is quite alright: I recommend a long woollen scarf for the job, but any piece of natural-fibre fabric will do. Again, I recommend you avoid using black.

CREATING A SPACE

The operation is best carried out at the time of the waxing Moon (see Chapter 6).

First, create a place or Vé where the working is to be made. You do this by performing rites of separation, purification and consecration. The rites can be as simple or as complex as you like, there are no strict rules governing these, just as long as you address the three prime issues. The ritual described below is my own personal method. Feel free to adapt it as required.

SEPARATION

The Vé represents a globe in space, half below the surface and half above. So the area you are going to mark out on the

For the rite of empowering a bindrune, you will need water, incense, a candle, a binding-cloth and a waxing moon.

DRAWING A CIRCLE

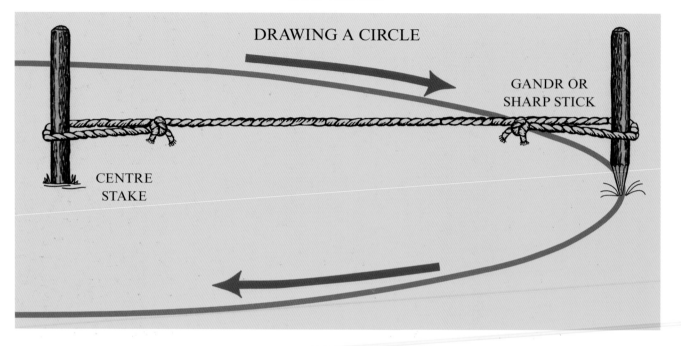

GANDR OR
SHARP STICK

CENTRE
STAKE

floor or ground will be a circle, which doesn't have to be geometrically perfect, but the closer you can get to it the better. If you are outdoors, you can mark the earth with your gandr or runic wand (see Chapter 6). If you don't have one, then use a stick of wood that has been sharpened to a point using a knife. If indoors, use chalk or some other material that will not cause damage to surfaces.

To inscribe a circle, place a permanent upright of some sort in the centre of your Vé (i.e. a stake pushed into the earth, or if indoors any heavy object that won't move). Now attach a length of string to it. The string should have a loop at each end and should be just the right length to reach the limit of your selected space. Now attach the string to your sharpened stick or the chalk, and walk around the area, keeping the string stretched taut and marking the ground or floor as you go.

Purification

First you must consecrate the water. Pour a few ounces into a clean jug or bowl. Wood is good, glass or ceramic is alright, but not plastic. Stir the water with the first finger of your writing hand in a clockwise direction, starting at the North, then East, South, West and back to North. This is called a 'sun-wise' rotation.

Then speak these words, or invent your own incantation:

In the name of Kauno, into this water I direct the power of the runes, that it will be pure and clean. In the service of all the gods, so must it be!

Now take a level teaspoonful or so of sea-salt and drop it from your hand into the water. Use the same finger to stir it sun-wise nine times, speaking this incantation, or one of your own devising:

In the name of Fehu, here is the salt of life to purify this Vé and keep it free from evil. In the service of all the gods, so must it be!

While you are doing this, close your eyes and try to imagine the energy flowing from your fingers into the water. Picture the energy as a bright light moving from your fingertips, through the water surface, then mingling with the clear waters. At the completion of the ninth rotation the consecration is complete.

You can now use the water to purify your Vé. Starting at the North and progressing sun-wise to East, South, West, then back to North, sprinkle the water with your fingers. At each compass point speak these or similar words:

With water and salt, I purify this sacred Vé.

Keep going around the circle until you have used up all the water, repeating the incantation at each point. Now stand in the centre of the Vé while you light the incense.

Take the incense around the circle, starting at the North and progressing sun-wise to each point. At every stop speak

these or similar words:

With fire and air, I purify this sacred Vé.

Two or three times around the rotation will be sufficient, but leave the incense burning at the centre of the Vé until it goes out by itself. Now your Vé is purified.

CONSECRATION

While the incense is still burning (light a new stick if the first one has gone out), carry your gandr or stick around the circle. At each point, speak these or similar words while pointing your gandr in the relevant compass direction:

At the North:
I call upon Jera and the power of completion. So must it be!

At the East:
I call upon Berkanan and the power of birth. So must it be!

At the South:
I call upon Dagaz and the power of daylight. So must it be!

At the West:
I call upon Kauno and the power of enlightenment. So must it be!

Then return to the centre of the Vé, face towards the North, point your gandr directly skyward and say:

I call upon the power of Mother Earth, Yggdrasil, the tree of the world, and Mjöllnir the weapon of Thor to consecrate this sacred Vé. In the service of all the Gods, so must it be!

As you do this, close your eyes again and envisage an image of the sky above your head as if it were a continuation of the sphere of the Vé. This is best done at night, but at any time try to imagine the dark of the night sky. As you watch it, bring to mind the 24 runes of the Futhark. Make them appear among the stars as bright, shining objects in a circle around you, as shown in the illustration on page 194.

When this image has become fixed in your imagination, then your Vé is complete and ready for use.

You may carry out the 'virtual' creation of a bindrune used as a tattoo, by tracing the outline of each rune within the bindrune with your finger dipped in the salty water. This can be painful in that the tattoo has not yet healed, and is not recommended in case of infection or other injury.

NORTH

NAMING THE BINDRUNE

Whether you are working with a tattoo or a solid object, choose a name for the bindrune. For example, your own name would be fitting for a personal bindrune made up of your initials, but any name of your own choosing would be acceptable for a practical bindrune.

You will certainly have more than one runic character in your design and you should address each rune in turn, starting at the top and/or right and working through to the bottom and/or left. Identify the outline of each individual rune within the bindrune. Trace the outline of each rune one at a time, speaking the name of the individual rune three times while you are tracing its outline.

Try to feel the power of each rune; let it surround you, enter your subconscious and take over your psyche. Then allow it to return to the design. After speaking the name of the last rune in the bind for the third time, but while still tracing it, speak the name of the bindrune itself: for example, 'Spiritual Warrior', 'Soul Healer', 'Protector',

OPPOSITE: Envisaging the 24 runes of the Futhark as bright, shining objects, forming a circle above you in the night sky.

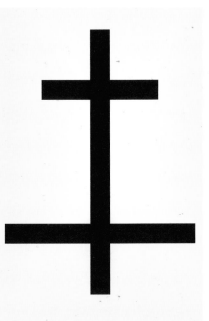

'Peacemaker'. If you have a more complex design that includes more than one bindrune, you must repeat this process for each rune in each bindrune.

As you speak this last phrase, visualize the power of the design surrounding your spiritual being. When you have finished, make the sign of Thor's Hammer (see above) over the design without touching it.

Now that you have completed this rite once for each bindrune, the object or tattoo must now be covered with a cloth so that all light is excluded from it.

Now be prepared and take things slowly, as you might easily become dizzy performing this next element of the rite. You must turn a full circle nine times. You need to find the East-West line in the place you are using, starting by facing East, then turning sun-wise towards the South, then West, then North and back to facing East. You may pause a few seconds between each turn, if necessary, giving you time to memorize the next lines appropriate to each part of the turn.

EMPOWERMENT

Now comes the empowerment. Speak these words as you complete the rotations:

*In the name of the gods and
goddesses of the earth, sky and
underworld,
And by the power of the four
elements,
I ward off evil spirits,
And all foul entities,
The demons who injure me,
Those that would weaken me, those
who would destroy my being,
Those who would attempt my
destruction,
I ward off all misfortunes and attacks
of evil intent,*

*From fearsome monsters and
meddlesome imps,
From tricksters and jealous rivals,
From ill omens and evil portents,
From malignant on-lays and laid air,
And from the ministrations of harmful
spirits,
May I be freed from all injury,
Let me be blessed with that which I
desire,
And with those attributes I seek,
In accordance with universal runic law,
And of my own choice and free will,*

So must it be. Ka!

You will notice there are 18 lines, so you must therefore speak two with each rotation. The final 'So must it be. Ka!' (meaning 'Let it be done') is spoken after the last two lines during the 9th rotation.

Now the object or tattoo must remain in darkness for a symbolic nine-fold period. This can be nine minutes, nine hours, nine days, etc. For a tattoo, let's be sensible here, 9 hours is the most anyone would want to undertake, but the length of time is your own decision. The longer the period of gestation, the greater the power will be, but you can always repeat the empowerment at a later date, should you feel that the influence has begun to fade.

SYMBOLIC BIRTH

Finally, you will bring the bindrune back into the light of day. This is the symbolic birth, and the bindrune is now emerging as a newborn entity. Speak the name of the bindrune while you are unwrapping the covering cloth, and complete a clockwise rotation starting at the East, just as you did during the empowerment rite.

Next, pure water should be applied to the surface of the object or tattoo by hand or with a natural cloth. With wooden amulets and the like, use the cloth and wipe the item dry immediately on completion of the rite. Speak these words as you apply the water:

*I spread water over thee
And name thee (the name of the object
or design)
By the power of Earth, Fire, Wind and
Water.*

And so must it be. Ka!

Now comes the final act. Touch the bindrune and speak these words with your fingers resting on it:

*Strong Warrior (or the name of the
bindrune) bearer of my will
Obey my command I beseech you
For the purpose of (speak the purpose
you have chosen)*

*May you do my will
Until your mission is complete
And in accordance with runic law*

And so must it be. Ka!

Now visualize three links in a chain. In your mind's eye you see these three links encircling the bindrune, and see the chain binding it to your psyche and to your subconscious. Then speak these words as you imagine that the desired purpose you have stated in the ritual has now been awakened and is working on your behalf.

*Now the working is complete
In which you have been formed
From the world of chaos
Into the world of men
In the name of the gods and goddesses
of the Earth, Sky and Underworld
And of my own choice and free will.*

So must it be. Ka!

That is the end of the rite. Your bindrune will now be fully empowered and will work for the stated purposes for the rest of your days; however, the influence does tend to fade with time and may at some time need refreshing with a repeat empowerment.

BINDRUNES

Disempowerment

If at any time you wish to disempower a bindrune amulet there is a particular way to do so.

There may be occasions when the owner of a bindrune amulet wishes to discontinue using it, or indeed prevent it from having any further effect. This can be achieved by a simple reversal rite that requires both the spiritual and physical destruction of the amulet.

The original empowerment rite was a multi-stage process performed at the time of creation as detailed above. The final stage of the process, involving the four elements of water, earth, fire and air, is the only part of the rite that requires reversal to complete the disempowerment. The elements are therefore addressed in the order of air, fire, earth and finally water.

Preparations and Equipment

First draw a sketch of the bindrune and take it with you when you perform the reversal rite.

The rite should be performed outdoors and in darkness. If you have a tree in your own backyard, then that is an ideal location, otherwise you will need to find a spot near to a tree where public access is possible. Choose a location where there are no restrictions on starting small fires. You must ensure you are following any local regulations regarding fires, making sure you carry out the recommended safety precautions.

You will need some equipment to start the fire, such as paper kindling and perhaps some barbecue starter or lighter fluid. You should also take a small container, such as a metal bowl or an old tin can with some holes punched in the bottom. This is to contain the fire and ensure that it cannot spread.

You will need a small scrap of natural fabric, such as cotton, linen or wool, that is big enough to wrap around the remains of the amulet. You will need a trowel or some other small digging implement to make a hole in the ground 6–10in (15–25cm) deep. You will also need a bottle of natural water as used for the empowerment (see above).

Select a quiet spot near the tree. It is not important what kind of tree you choose, but if you do have a choice I recommend you touch the trunk of a few different trees until you find one that feels 'right' to you. Keep trying until you find one that gives you some kind of positive reaction to your touch. A feeling of well-being, satisfaction or comfort would be an acceptable spiritual reaction, while a warm or comfortable tactile sensation would be a good physical indicator. There is no need for a witness, but women in particular are advised not to go unaccompanied into a secluded area at night.

The Disempowerment Rite

This first stage of the rite addresses the power of the first element: air. Having found a suitable spot, remove any metal objects from the wrist and fingers of your left hand (or your right hand if you happen to be left-handed). Take the bindrune in the palm of your non-writing hand and curl your fingers around it to make a 'tube', with the amulet lodged in the middle. Touch the tree with your writing hand and maintain contact with it during the incantation. Breathe three times into the tube of your fingers so that your breath passes over and around the amulet. Then speak these words:

Oh runic amulet, bringer of
(speak the purpose of the amulet here)
Now your work is done.
I thank you and the gods for your service.

Breathe another three times into the tube of your finger, then continue to speak:

You may return to Erda
(Erda being the runic name for Mother

Earth, pronounced *ERD-THA)*

   And assume again your formless state.
   So must it be, Ka!

   With the word 'Ka!' (let it be done)
breathe a final three times on the amulet.
You can now break contact with the tree.

   The second stage is to undo the work
of fire. Now the amulet must be burned
so that the marking can no longer be
distinguished. It is not necessary to
reduce the entire amulet to ash, although
that would be quite acceptable. It only
has to be sufficiently charred so that the
runic marking is obliterated. When this
has been achieved, extinguish the fire and
if necessary douse the remains using
some of the water.

   In the third stage you will reverse
the power of the earth. Tip out the
remains of the amulet onto the piece of
natural cloth and wrap them up. Dig a
hole 6–10in deep at the base of the tree,
within 2–3ft of the trunk, and place the
wrapped remains in the hole. Fill the hole
in and smooth the soil down with your
foot, so that it is level with the
surrounding ground.

   In this final stage the water must be
used to obliterate all traces of the
bindrune. By referring to the drawing you
made earlier, use a stick or your digging
implement to mark the design of the

amulet on the tamped-down earth over the burial spot. Make it no more than a few inches across, just big enough so that the design can be seen to be the same as that of the actual amulet. Now sprinkle the remaining water onto the marking on the earth so that it too becomes obliterated. You may use the fingers of your non-writing hand to help the water destroy the marks, if necessary.

With the first three stages of the rite now completed you have returned the physical manifestation of the amulet to the earth, but this final act is required to return its spiritual presence to the ether.

The last remnant of the bindrune remains only as a drawing on your piece of paper, and that should be completely burned over the patch of damp earth where the ashes of the amulet are buried.

This completes the disempowerment rite. I wish you Auja (good fortune)!

GANDR MAGIC

CHAPTER SIX
GANDR MAGIC

INTRODUCTION

The gandr is a short length of wood used to perform runic magic. It equates to the Wiccan instrument known popularly as a wand and is not to be confused with the runestaff. In ancient times a runestaff would have been the height of a man and was carried as a badge of office in much the same way as a bishop's mitre.

The wood used in the making of a gandr contains the vital essence of the tree from which the wood originated. A good guide to tree lore is, *Tree Wisdom*, by Jacqueline Memory Patterson, and I often refer to this excellent book.

The gandr is traditionally the length of the forearm – usually about 12–15in (30–40cm).

USING A GANDR

The gandr represents the power of the mind and may be used to move energy from one place to another, to create a spiritual state of consciousness, and to set up a Vé, i.e. a sacred rune-work area. It may also be used to combine energies in

specific patterns. It is an excellent tool for use in magic, healing, protection, and in exerting power over the elements.

EMPOWERMENT

The gandr must be fully empowered by runic ritual. The place for the empowerment, the day of the year, the time of night and phase of the moon, should be chosen carefully. Herbs, incense, sea-salt, natural water, earth, smoke and fire are used in this empowerment process. The rite suggested in the previous chapter may be adapted for this purpose.

You may prime the gandr for a particular magical working (a spell) by mental concentration and invoking the spirits of the appropriate gods, the purpose of this practice being to imbue

LEFT: A personal gandr (runic wand) made of ash (genus Fraxinus).

OPPOSITE: A gandr made from cotoneaster (genus Cotoneaster).

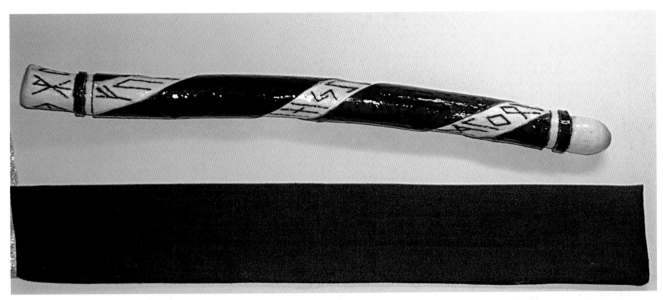

the gandr with the god's individual attributes. To do this you must be in harmony with the gods, asking them to share their power with the gandr. Imagine that power in your mind's eye, then initiate the movement of the raw energy entering into the gandr by breathing in and exhaling along the length of the wand.

The ninefold rule applies here. Carrying out the procedure nine times is the minimum, but the more multiples of nine you undertake the more effective the process will be. Your breath and focused attention are the means by which the power of the gods travel from the spiritual ether into the gandr. Think about what you will be using it for and how it will help you during the entire process.

MAGICAL FUNCTIONS

The natural mental progression is from intention and expectation to desire and then to action. These are the three steps to magic. They provide a straightforward path that moves the energy you have created in your mind from initiation, to formulation and completion. You can use this process in any magical workings, but it is essential to be clear about your intentions, i.e., what do you expect to achieve from the exercise? The critical factor is that you should genuinely want and need the result you seek.

Think about your situation when you have achieved the objective, feel it in your heart, not in the practical part of your conscious mind, but deep in your psyche. Experience that future situation where the magic has worked, and look at it from all points of view. If you concentrate on this task hard enough, and with sufficient belief, it will eventually emerge as an actuality. At that stage you must pause and ask yourself, is this right?, is it wise?, is it what I need? If you are convinced the answer to

205

all these questions is yes, then you are ready for the next stage.

In this next step you should create a single concept in your mind, combining the desires and expectations, the presence of the gods, and the mental reality of your completed objective. This concept becomes something variously known as the 'Force', the 'Entity', or the 'One Power', but I call it the 'Meld', because it blends and combines the input of several sources while fulfilling a single function. It is the realization of the source energies, which you may now deploy by your own physical and mental actions through the use of the gandr.

Allow the Meld to completely suffuse your mental state. Let it encompass your intuition, expectation and desire. Imagine yourself releasing the power of the Meld from your mind. Concentrate on that single idea and you will reach the stage where the Meld achieves an existence of its own that is as real as yourself. You can't see it or touch it, but you must be able to feel it, and when that happens you will be able to direct it.

All magical traditions use the concept of blending energies, working them into a desired form, and eventually directing them to carry out a required task. Creation of the Meld is the basic component of any successful magical working.

THE FOUR DIRECTIONS

The power of the four directions should always be addressed for a successful result. When invoking the help of the gods, or empowering an object to carry out a magical function, you may use your gandr to point in the appropriate directions, thus directing the energy of the Meld.

The North represents Odin, and the three Norns, Urd, Verdandi and Skuld. Objects associated with the North are Odin's spear, Gungnir, and the Norns' threads of fate. The ruling rune is Jera.

The East is the domain of Frigg (Frigga) and Tiw. Frigg's distaff and Tiw's battle sword are the associated objects and Berkanan is the ruling rune.

The South calls up Thor and Iduna, Thor's hammer, Mjöllnir, and the golden apples of Iduna being the appropriate objects. Dagaz is the ruling rune.

OPPOSITE: The three Norns or Fates, as represented in a performance of Wagner's Ring Cycle.

LEFT: Freya, Frigg's sister, and the goddess of love, beauty and fertility.

BELOW: Frigg (Frigga or Fricka), the consort of the god Odin (Wotan).

The West is the direction of Freya and Njord, the associated objects being Freya's necklace and Njord's axe. The ruling rune is Kauno.

THE EIGHT DIVISIONS OF THE YEAR

Timing is critical in any magical working, for if the appropriate energies are lacking, the magic will be unlikely to succeed. One might as well try to put a broken egg back together again – it can't be done. But with the correct timing, your magical working can achieve wonders.

The eight divisions of the year represent the traditional annual cycle of northern Europe. The best times for runic magic are the eight seasonal solar festivals, each having their own traditions that have been passed down through the ages.

The days of power occur at the equinoxes, solstices, and the four cross-quarter days. The following list will assist you in selecting an appropriate day on which to carry out your magical function.

These names and dates are related to the Northern Hemisphere; for users in the Southern Hemisphere the festivals occur on the same dates, but the names and associations are reversed.

SAMHAIN, OCTOBER 31. Colours: black, red and orange. Plants associated with it are corn (maize), pumpkins, gourds, apples and corn stalks. Ruling runes: Wunjo, Hagalaz, Naudiz.

OPPOSITE: Pine cones are associated with Yule, and corn (maize) with Samhain.

RIGHT & BELOW: Spring flowers are linked with Eostre (Easter), and cherries with Imbolc.

YULE, DECEMBER 20–23 (winter solstice). Colours: red and green; plants are the Yule Log, mistletoe, holly, pine and pine cones, and any type of nut. Ruling runes: Isa, Jera, Ihwaz.

IMBOLC OR CANDLEMAS, FEBRUARY 2. Colours: red and white; plants are roses, cherries and apples. Ruling runes: Perth, Algiz, Sowilo.

EOSTRE, MARCH 20–23 (spring equinox). Colours: green, white and silver. Plants are all spring flowers and seeds. Coloured eggs are a token. Ruling runes: Tiwaz, Ehwaz, Berkanan.

BELTANE, MAY 1–5. The complete spectrum of colour is associated with Beltane, as are all flowers, garlands, trees, and fresh leaves. Ruling runes: Mannaz, Laguz, Ingwaz.

LITHA, JUNE 20–23 (summer solstice). The colour of Litha is green, and plants associated with this day are roses, vines, and leaves. Ruling runes: Othila, Dagaz, Fehu.

ABOVE: Flowers in general are associated with Beltane.

OPPOSITE: Roses and vines are linked with Litha.

Lughnassad(h), August 1. Also called Lammas. Colours: green, yellow, and red. Plants are corn, grains, tomatoes, berries and flowers. Ruling runes: Uruz, Thurisaz, Ansuz.

Mabon, September 20–23 (autumn equinox). The colours of Mabon are orange, brown, yellow and red. All crops

OPPOSITE & LEFT: Wheat. grains and berries are linked with Lughnassad.

are associated with this festival, as are the brilliant fall of leaves around this time. Ruling runes: Raido, Kauno, Gebo.

The ancients understood the phases of the Moon and their significance in our daily lives. They knew the waxing Moon was the time for building energy, while the waning Moon was the time for releasing it. From the new Moon to the first-quarter Moon is a time to initiate and build, to clarify your intention and expectation. From the first quarter to the full Moon is the time to cultivate what you have created and to gather the energy needed for its successful completion.

The full Moon is called the High Moon, because it is then that lunar energies are strongest. The last quarter of the Moon corresponds to harvest time, when you reap the rewards of your efforts. The last quarter, through the dark Moon and into the new Moon, is a time to explore the mysteries of life, rebirth, and dreams. When doing magic with

OPPOSITE: All the autumnal colours are associated with Mabon.

RIGHT: The Crescent Moon is linked with Algiz.

PAGES 216–217: The Full Moon is associated with Litha and the rune Dagaz.

runes, select the phase of the Moon that corresponds to the magical function you are working.

The following indicates the eight-fold Moon phase cycle and how it relates to the days of power, together with the primary corresponding rune.

• The New Moon is linked with the Yule Festival and the rune Jera.
• The Crescent Moon is linked with Imbolc and the rune Algiz.
• The First Quarter Moon is linked with Eostre and the rune Berkanan.
• The Gibbous Moon is linked with Beltane and the rune Laguz.
• The Full Moon is linked with Litha and the rune Dagaz.
• The Decreasing Moon is linked with Lughnassad and the rune Thurisaz.
• The Last Quarter Moon is linked with Mabon and the rune Kauno.

• The Dark Moon is linked with Samhain and the rune Hagalaz.

THE FIVE ELEMENTS

Using the elements of earth (north), air (east), fire (south), and water (west or all directions), with the fifth element being spirit (centre), is a concept that may also enhance your magical function.

Because of their harsh environment, the ancients placed ice at the north and earth at the centre. The elements of earth, air, fire, and water/ice may thus be combined with your workings. Use these runes to call upon the elemental energies:
• Earth: Wunjo, Jera, Berkanan, Ihwaz, Ehwaz, Ingwaz, Othila
• Air: Ansuz, Raido, Gebo, Algiz, Tiwaz, Mannaz, Ihwaz
• Fire: Sowilo, Fehu, Thurisaz, Kauno, Naudiz, Dagaz, Ihwaz
• Water/Ice: Uruz, Laguz, Perth, Hagalaz, Isa, Ihwaz

You can improve your empathy with the elements by associating them with your physical attributes. When invoking this aspect of the working, bear in mind your relationship with the elements. The more you practise this, the closer your attunement and the more effective your magic will be. Here is a chant that will help you do this:

My flesh and bones are the earth.
The earth is my flesh and bones.
We are one.

My breath is the air.
The air is my breath.
We are one.

My potential is thawing ice.
The thawing ice is my potential.
We are one.

My eyes are the light.
The light is my eyes.
We are one.

Water and ice are associated with the runes Uruz, Laguz, Perth, Hagalaz, Isa, Ihwaz.

RUNE TRANSCRIPTION

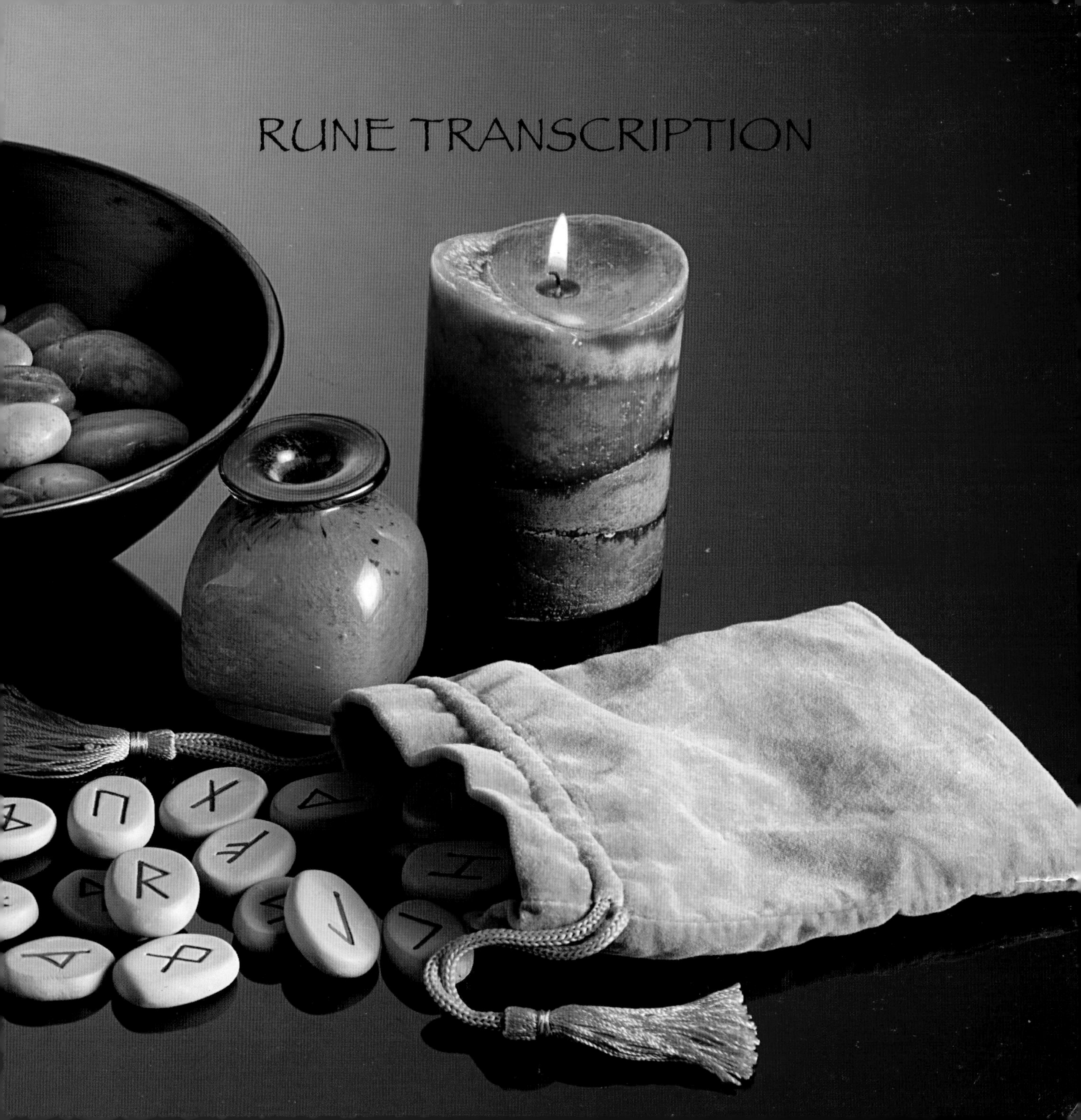

RUNE TRANSCRIPTION

THE DIFFERENCE BETWEEN TRANSLATION & TRANSCRIPTION

I am frequently asked about writing in runes by people wanting to represent their names in runes, write secret or cryptic messages, create runic inscriptions or spells, and there are a dozen other reasons. One of the big misconceptions is that runes is a language and that one first has to translate modern English (or indeed any other modern language) into runes before writing. This is not the case.

The runes have no parallel in language. They are simply a system of writing, so you can write any word you can say using runes instead of the letters of the modern alphabet that we use to write English. Just think of the runes as an alternative ancient alphabet – the Futhark of 24 runes – instead of an alphabet of 26 letters.

There is no need to 'translate' anything, for it will sound the same whatever writing system you use. Just as the letters we call English (though actually they are Roman) are not in any language, because they are used in scores of languages, so it is the same with Arabic script, which is used in dozens of different languages, and the Cyrillic

BELOW: Runic and Roman characters on a stone carving from the Historiska Museet, Stockholm.

script, which is used in half a dozen more. This also pertains to the runes in that they can be used to write any language you choose.

The original users did have their own different languages – Scythian, Teutonic, Saxon, Danish, Norse, and eventually Old English or Anglo-Saxon. So there is no reason why runes can't be used for any language you like, including modern English. The only thing to remember is

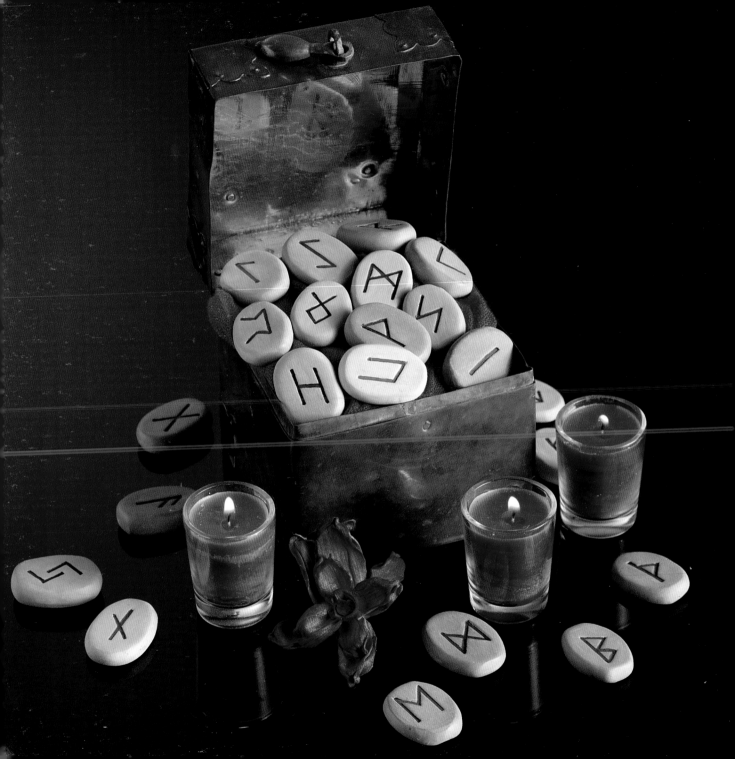

that the runes are phonetics, so that you write things the way they sound, not the way in which they are spelled. Because runes do not follow English spelling, the act of changing written English words into written runic words is called 'transcribing' and the process is known as 'transcription', a Latin-based word that literally means 'cross-writing'.

SOME INTRODUCTORY NOTES ON RUNIC TRANSCRIPTION

Transcribing modern letters into runes isn't as easy as one might think because the ancients didn't use the same sounds as we do today. In fact they had some we don't use, and we have some they didn't have. In any case, here is a table (right) giving my own rendering of the letter equivalents of each rune:

EXTRA RUNES ADDED BY THE ANGLO-SAXONS

The Anglo-Saxons, who used runes in Britain, gradually increased their number to 33 (some experts say the total reached 38 eventually) by inventing new runes to represent new sounds. This is because there were changes in the way people spoke over the centuries. This always occurs in written languages, and it's happening to modern English right now.

Rune	Name	Letter Equivalent	Sound
ᚠ	Fehu	F	F as in fat
ᚢ	Uruz	U	U as in under or OO as in fool
ᚦ	Thurisaz	Th	Th diphthong as in thin, or in weather
ᚨ	Ansuz	A	A as in add
ᚱ	Raido	R	R as in red
ᚲ	Kauno	C (hard), K	C as in cat; K as in king
ᚷ	Gebo	G	G as is good; Gh as in loch
ᚹ	Wunjo	W, V	W as in wax; v as in van
ᚺ	Hagalaz	H	H as in hat
ᚾ	Naudiz	N	N as in now
ᛁ	Isa	I (short)	I as in sit
ᛃ	Jera	J, Y	J as in jam; Y as in yap
ᛇ	Ihwaz	I (long)	I as in site, Y as in style
ᛈ	Perth	P	P as in pot
ᛉ	Algiz	Z	Z as in zone. S as in cousin (may also have been the rolling RRR heard in Scottish dialect)
ᛊ	Sowilo	C (soft), S	C as in nice; S as sit
ᛏ	Tiwaz	T	T as in top
ᛒ	Berkanan	B	B as in bag
ᛗ	Ehwaz	E	E as in end
ᛖ	Mannaz	M	M as in man
ᛚ	Laguz	L	L as in let
ᛜ	Ingwaz	Ng	Ng diphthong as in finger or ring
ᛟ	Othila	O	O as in old, or in cot
ᛞ	Dagaz	D	D as in dog

LEFT: Runic carving on a 12th-century stone font, now in the Historiska Museet, Stockholm.

OPPOSITE: A runestone from the Domkyrka (cathedral) of Uppsala, Sweden.

GH followed by a residual E vowel (listen to an Irishman or a Scot say 'loch' and you'll know what I mean). So 'through' would have sounded more like 'thrucher' and 'sigh' would have been 'sicher', which is far too difficult for lazy English tongues! So the sound gradually faded away and remains only in our curious spelling system. It is becoming quite common nowadays to abbreviate 'through' to 'thru' and I am wondering how long it will be before it becomes an acceptable spelling with an entry in Websters, or perhaps, perish the thought, even the Oxford English Dictionary.

There is another language characteristic that has an effect on transcription. Over quite short periods of time, people start abbreviating common words that are too long for comfort. The new words start out as slang and eventually become adopted as words in their own right. Two common examples of this are the words 'bus' and 'pram'.

Words change, people get lazy with their pronunciation, and gradually, almost imperceptibly, vowel sounds become flattened or altered. Just take the word 'colour' as an example. This word originated from the Latin *color*, but as it progressed through Middle English through Norman French to English became *caloure, couleur* and colour. When I was young, people used to say 'coll-ore', but now it is more usually 'cullur', the short U sound being easier to articulate than the short O and long O of the original word. In American English, the spelling has reverted to the original *color*, just as the U has been dropped in other similar words with a Latin root, while the stick-in-the-mud Brits are still spelling it the old way, but saying it in the new, to the confusion of colonials and foreigners alike.

Another thing that happens is that hard consonants at the end of words get softened or completely dropped. Good examples of this are words like 'through' and 'sigh', where the GH ending is no longer sounded. The Anglo-Saxons pronounced those words with a guttural

Bus started out as *omnibus*, a Latin word meaning 'all', in this case indicating a vehicle that was for the use of all, but within 20 years of its introduction, lazy Londoners had dropped the first four letters of the word. Within a very short time even the apostrophe, indicating that letters had been discarded, was dropped and it must be at least 50 years since bus became accepted as a proper word.

Much the same happened with the word 'perambulator', indicating 'an object being walked or pushed by someone walking'. But again, laziness shortened the word to 'peram', and by the beginning of the 20th century, even the first E vowel had disappeared, and pram also entered the dictionary as a word in its own right.

FIRST TRANSCRIPTION EXERCISE

To demonstrate the phonetic value of runes as opposed to modern English letters, let's take the word 'thing' as an example. The TH sound is represented by just one rune – Thurisaz – instead of the two runes representing T and H, so you write Thurisaz, not Tiwaz with Hagalaz. And for the same reason, the NG sound is represented by the single rune Ingwaz, and not Naudiz with Gebo. Therefore, the word 'thing' written in runes is Thurisaz Isa Ingwaz. So you can see how runes are

DISCOVERING RUNES

LEFT: These runestones, most of which are from the 11th century, litter the ground around Uppsala Cathedral in Sweden.

BELOW: The word 'thing' spelled out in runes.

written from what you hear, not from what you see, which is what 'phonetic' means.

The first step in transcribing anything into runes is to write the word down in normal English. Then go through the words and change them into a phonetic form. If you find it hard to dispense with the conventions of modern spelling, say the words out loud and write them down, possibly as would a five-year-old child. Suppose we were to transcribe HAVE A HAPPY BIRTHDAY, RINGO into runes. I don't actually know anybody called Ringo personally, but it's a good name to use for this example because it contains the NG sound.

So let us start by breaking down the sentence phonetically: HAV A HAPY BIR(th)DAY RI(ng)O. The first thing you notice is that I have removed the silent E from the end of HAVE, because there is no need to transcribe silent letters since they have no sound value. Next you will see that I have reduced the double P in HAPPY to a single letter, in that as far as the sound of the word is concerned, the second P is quite superfluous. Next, you see that I have put the TH of BIRTHDAY into brackets (th), because the two letters are going to become the single rune, Thurisaz, when we transcribe.

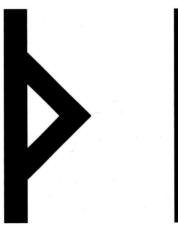

There is actually a symbol for this in phonetics, which you will see in dictionaries, where you are shown how to pronounce words. It looks like this, þ. See how similar this symbol is to the rune Thurisaz? That's because it is Thurisaz, or at least it's a modern representation of the ancient rune. Phoneticists call it 'thorn', which is a modern translation of one of the rune's ancient names.

The phonetic symbol for the NG sound is ŋ, the right-hooked en, but in this case does not derive from any runic form. For the same reason, where they appear in RINGO, I have bracketed the N and the G together like this (ng); they are going to be transcribed as the single rune Ingwaz.

If you look at the above you will see that the message has now been fully transcribed.

You will have to make your own mind up concerning diphthong vowels, i.e. vowel sounds where English uses two letters tied together as in ai, ea, oa, ie, oi and so on. The ancients were very individual in the way they represented these; some wrote two-vowel runes, some combined the two runes into a bindrune, and others simply used the nearest rune to the sound they wanted. You might find examples in runic inscriptions where the word 'aid' is written as below, or with Ansuz and Ihwaz combined to form a bindrune (see opposite above left).

In summary then, you simply substitute runes for each letter of the

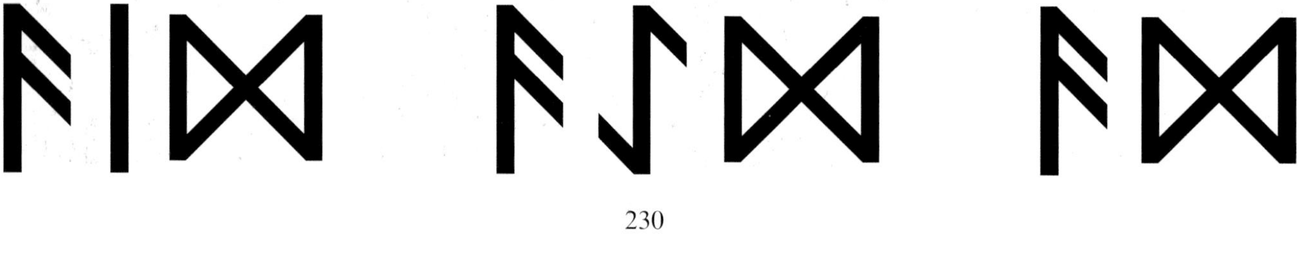

phonetic message or name and put a space between each.

PUNCTUATION AND DIRECTION

The ancients didn't always leave spaces and they didn't actually have any punctuation marks, but there are a number of runic inscriptions that use a colon-type mark, and some coins where a small Maltese-type cross was used to separate words. So, if you think it will make your message easier to read, by all means use a simple form of punctuation.

The examples I have given are written from left-to-right, the same way we write modern English. But the ancients were not so particular about direction. There are numerous examples of them writing from right-to-left, and there are a few examples of 'continuous stave' writing, which was writing left-to-

One of the 11th-century runestones at Jarlabanke's Bridge, Uppland, Sweden.

RUNE TRANSCRIPTION

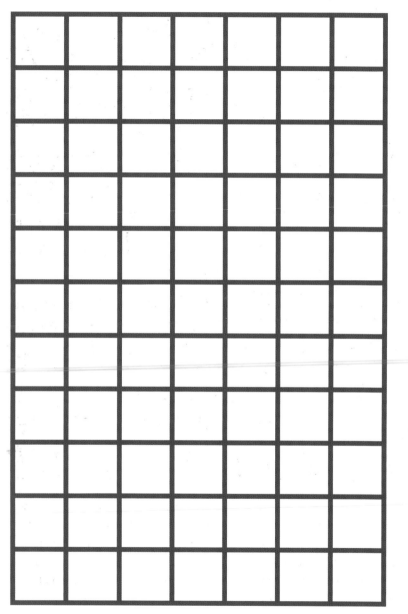

LEFT: *A grid layout for drawing runes.*

OPPOSITE: *A runestone at Bække, Denmark.*

right on the first line, then right-to-left on the next, and so on, making the passage continuous but reversing direction every line, as you would move your counter in the game of Snakes and Ladders.

There are a few odd examples of writing vertically, both downwards and upwards, and I know of one runestone in Stockholm, Sweden, where the writing follows the outline of a writhing snake, so that some of the inscription is in fact upside-down.

So don't feel that your runic transcription has to follow the left-to-right rules of modern English. Have fun and experiment a little!

RUNE FONTS
If you want to write runic messages using your computer, you will need to install a rune font on your system. There is a selection of free fonts gathered from the worldwide web that you may download from one of my websites at www.rune-fonts.co.uk. Most of the free fonts I discovered on the web had

something wrong with them, so I designed a variety of fonts myself to use on my websites and which are also available for download at modest cost. To the best of my knowledge they are complete and accurate.

If you are sending runic messages to someone else electronically, they must also have the same font as yours installed on their system to see the message as you wrote it. If they don't, the programmes Word, Excel, Outlook, or any Windows-based application, will render your work using the computer's default font, usually Times, Courier, Arial or Helvetica, so that all they will see is a mixture of the original English and a mish-mash of strange characters.

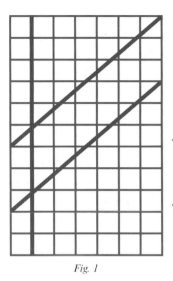

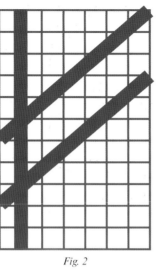

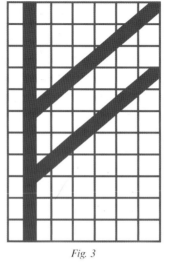

Fig. 1   *Fig. 2*   *Fig. 3*   *Fig. 4*

How To Draw Runes

Runes were originally cut into wood using a knife and they were then made up of straight lines, because curves are hard to execute with a straight blade. The lines were all vertical or angled, and there were no horizontal lines.

As time went by and technology developed, it became possible to carve runes into bone, stone, metal and many other materials. In fact, most of the rune relics we have today are on these more durable materials. So when monument-makers in the dark ages began to carve runic inscriptions using chisels, they were inclined to employ a modicum of artistic license, changing the rune shapes slightly,

incorporating a few curves here and there, and making their inscriptions a little more attractive or fashionable.

But the pure form of the runes consists of straight vertical and angled lines, so that is where we shall begin, but feel free to give rein to your own artistic impulses at a later stage.

To simplify matters we will use a grid made up of squares and draw any angled lines at 45°. Whether you are working on paper or are using computer graphics, this means you can get the angled lines by joining up the corners of the squares.

The grid should be roughly in the proportion 2:3, in other words if it's 2

inches wide, it should be about 3 inches tall. This one happens to be 7 squares wide and 11 tall, but you can use any size you like (see page 232).

ABOVE: Diagram showing the stages of development of a rune drawing.

OPPOSITE ABOVE: Three examples of the grid being used to compose runes of different shapes.

OPPOSITE BELOW: Computer-generated graphics use special effects to eenhance runic characters.

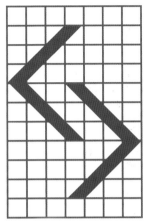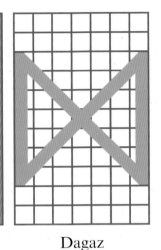

Jera	Mannaz	Dagaz

filters to the design, producing more attractive, individual effects as a result.

This is the same basic method I have been using for composing bindrune designs for many years. Of course, you can refine the process for speed and convenience by developing templates and a database of pre-defined objects in most graphic applications. These are very useful if, like me, you intend to produce a large number of designs.

NOW LET'S DRAW OUR FIRST RUNE, FEHU From Fig. 1 (opposite) you will have noticed that I didn't use the whole grid, because I wanted the angled lines to go through the box corners. In Fig. 2 the strokes have been thickened, and in Fig. 3 the edges have been tidied up. Finally, in Fig. 4, the grid has been removed, leaving a perfectly proportioned Fehu rune.

When you are experimenting with the other runes, you will find that some shapes, like Mannaz, fit the whole 7 x 11 grid, but others do not fit it too well. For example, Jera uses only 7 x 9 of the grid and Dagaz is easier to draw using only 7 x 7.

I sometimes wonder whether the old rune-carvers used a similar method,

because both Jera and Dagaz often appear shorter than the other runes in ancient Futharks.

For users of computer graphics, these stark geometric patterns can now be enhanced by applying colour and various

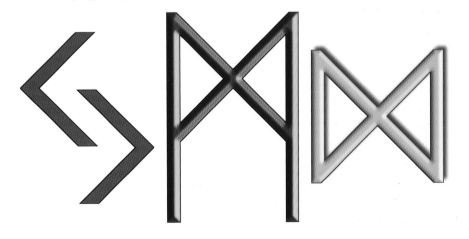

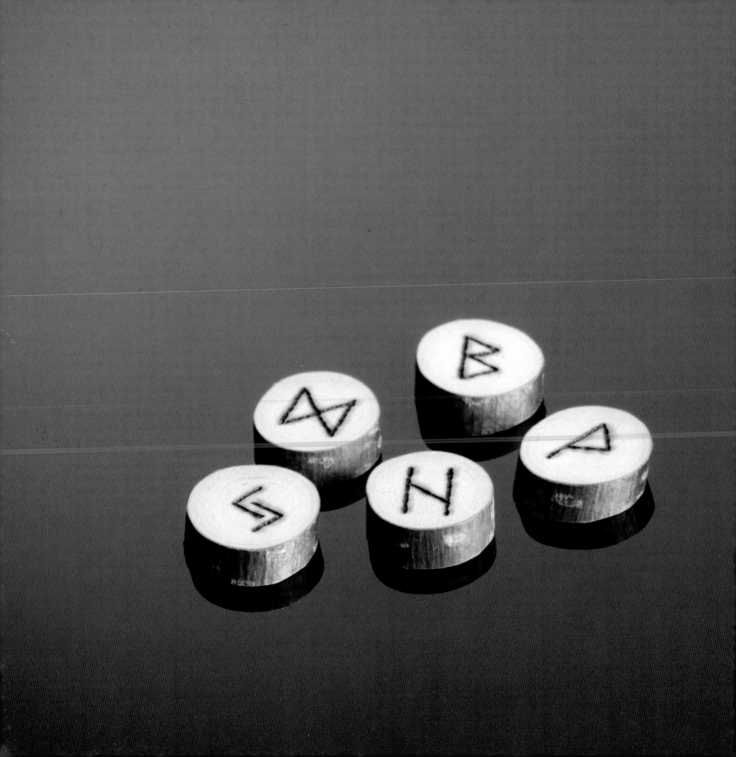

BIBLIOGRAPHY

RUNIC ARCHAEOLOGY

Runes: An Introduction
Ralph M.V. Elliott
Manchester University Press, Manchester,
UK, 1959

An Introduction to English Runes
Dr R.I. Page
Methuen, London, UK, 1973

Reading the Past - Runes
Dr R.I. Page
British Museum Publications, London,
UK, 1987

The Runes of Sweden
S.B.F. Jansson
Phoenix House, London, UK, 1962

Runes and their Origin
E. Moltke
Nationalmuseets Forlag, Copenhagen,
Denmark, 1981

Handbook of the Old Nordic Runic
Monuments of Scandinavia and
England
Dr George Stephens
Llanerch Reprints, Fellinfach, UK, 1993
(originally published by Williams &
Northgate, London, 1884)

MAGIC, RUNE MAGIC AND RUNIC
DIVINATION

The Tree: The Complete Book of Saxon
Witchcraft
Raymond Buckland
Samuel Weiser, York Beach, Maine, USA,
1974

Leaves of Yggdrasil
Freya Aswynn
Llewellyn, St Paul, Minnesota, USA, 1990

Northern Mysteries and Magic
Freya Aswynn
Llewellyn, St Paul, Minnesota, USA, 1998

Power and Principles of the Runes
Freya Aswynn
Thoth Publications, Loughborough, UK,
2007

The Way of Wyrd
Brian Bates
Hutchinson, London, UK, 1983

Rune Magic
Nigel Pennick
Harper Collins, London, UK, 1992

Book of Talismans
Willam Thomas & Kate Pavitt
Studio Editions, London, 1993

Spells, Charms, Talismans and Amulets
Pamela Ball
Arcturus, Leicester, UK, 2001

Complete Illustrated Guide to Runes
Nigel Pennick
Element Books, Shaftesbury, UK, 1999

Futhark: A Handbook of Rune Magic
Edred Thorsson
Samuel Weiser, York Beach, Maine, 1984

Runelore
Edred Thorsson
Samuel Weiser, York Beach, Maine, 1987

The Magic of the Runes
Michael Howard
Samuel Weiser, York Beach, Maine, 1980

The Runes & Other Magic Alphabets
Michael Howard
Aquarian, Dartford, UK, 1978

Rune Power
Kenneth Meadows
Element Books, Shaftesbury, UK, 1996

Runelore: A Handbook of Esoteric Runology
Edred Thorsson
Samuel Weiser, York Beach, Maine, 1984

The Rune Primer
Sweyn Plowright
Rune Net, Sydney, Australia, 2007

LANGUAGE, LINGUISTICS

Anglo-Saxon Verse Runes
Louis J Rodrigues
Llanerch Reprints Fellinfach, UK, 1992

Sweet's Anglo-Saxon Reader
Dorothy Whitelock
Oxford University Press, Oxford, UK, 1933

Old English
Leslie Blakeley
English Universities Press, London, UK, 1964

An Anglo-Saxon Dictionary
Dr Joseph Bosworth
Clarendon Press, London, UK, 1898. See also **The Anglo-Saxon Chronicles** below

HISTORY

The Dark Ages
David Talbot Rice (Ed.)
Thames & Hudson, London, UK. 1965

Introduction to Anglo-Saxon England
Peter Hunter Blair
Cambridge University Press, Cambridge, UK, 1959

Anglo-Saxon England
Sir Frank Stenton
Oxford University Press, Oxford, 1943

A History of the Anglo-Saxons
R H Hodgkin
Oxford University Press, Oxford, UK, 1952

The Anglo-Saxon Chronicles
G N Garmonsway
Dent, London, UK, 1953

BIBLIOGRAPHY

Viking Achievement
P G Foote & D M Wilson
Sidgwick & Jackson, London, 1970

Technology in the Time of the Vikings
Peter Hicks
Wayland Publishers, Hove, UK, 1997

The Vikings in Britain
H R Lloyn
Anchor Press, Tiptree, UK, 1977

Viking Age England
Julian D Richards
B T Batsford, Manchester, UK, 1981

NATURAL HISTORY

Our British Trees
Francis George Heath
Hutchinson & Co, Aylesbury, UK, 1907

The Countryside Companion
Tom Stephenson
Odhams Press, London, UK, 1931

The Complete Book of Herbs
A Clevely & K Richmond
Anness Publishing, London, UK, 1994

The Secret Life of Trees
Colin Tudge
Allen Lane, London, UK, 2005

LORE AND MYTHOLOGY

The Golden Bough
Sir J Fraser
MacMillan, London, UK, 1922

The Lost Gods of England
B Branston
Thames & Hudson, London, UK, 1957

An Introduction to Viking Mythology
John Grant
Grange Books, London, UK, 1997

Gods and Heroes from Viking Mythology
Brian Branston & Giovanni Caselli
Eurobook, London, UK, 1978

Pears Encyclopaedia of Myths and Legends
Sheila Savill (Ed.)
Pelham Books, London, UK, 1977

The Poetic Edda
Carolyne Larrington
Oxford University Press, Oxford, UK, 1996

The Edda of Snorri Sturluson
Anthony Kaulkes
Dent, London, UK, 1995

Tree Wisdom
Jacqueline Memory Paterson
Harper Collins, London, UK, 1996

OTHER SUBJECTS

The Old Straight Track
Alfred Watkins
Methuen, London, UK, 1925

Lines on the Landscape
Nigel Pennick & Paul Devereux
Robert Hale, London, UK, 1989

The Ley Hunters Companion
Paul Devereux & Ian Thompson
Thames & Hudson, London, UK, 1975

Crystals and Crystal Healing
Simon Lilly
Sebastian Kelly, Oxford, UK, 1998

INDEX

A

Algiz 55, 124–125, 209, 215, 218

Alruna 25

Amulets (see Bindrunes)

Anglo-Friesian Futhark 18, 59, 64
(see also Anglo Saxon Futhorc)

Anglo-Saxon Futhorc 17, 18, 20, 59,
61, 64

Ansuz 18, 25, 55, 80–81, 164, 218,
230

Aquarius 101

Aries 69

B

Baldr 129

Beltane 210, 215

Berkanan 14, 40, 58, 65, 136, 137, 206,
210, 215, 218

Bewcastle Cross, the 54

Bible, the 12

Bindrunes, the 171, 182–201, 230,
235
as amulets 182, 188, 198, 200, 201
as monograms 183, 184
as tattoos 182, 183, 188, 193, 197
disempowerment of 198
disempowerment rite 198, 200, 201
empowerment of 195, 197
empowerment rite 188, 190 188
naming the 195
practical bindrunes 184, 187, 188
separating the 190, 192
sequestering the 188
symbolic birth of 197

Blank rune, the 58, 59 58,
164–165

Bragi the Skald 17, 21

Broby bro runestones *62, 63*

Bronze Age runes 12, 14

Buddhism 51

C

Calendars or almanacs, runic 30

Cancer 125, 153

Candlemas (see Imbolc)

Capricorn 105

Casting the runes 34–51
Germania Cast 40
Nine-Rune Cast 41

Celtic Crosses 45
Ardboe Cross, the *46–47*

Cunebald's Cross 29, 30

D

Dagaz 160–161, 184, 206, 210, 215,
218, 235

Days of power 208, 215

Divination 12, 14, 15, 17, 18, 25, 34–51
casting the runes 34–51
choice of subjects 34
preparing for 34, 36, 37 34

questions asked in 34

divining systems 37

spreads used in 37, 40, 41, *41*, 42, 43, 45, 48, 49, 50, 51:

  Nine Worlds of Yggdrasil 51

  Eightfold Wheel 51

  Five Directions Spread 49

  Odin's Rune 43

  Quest for Truth Spread 45, 49 45

  Runic Cross 45

  Thor's Hammer Spread 50, 51

  Three Lifetimes Spread 48, 49

  Three-Rune Spread 43

Divisions of the year (see under Beltane, Imbolc, Litha, Lughnassad(h), Mabon, Samhain, Yule)

Domkyrka, Uppsala runestone *227*

Dowsing with a runic pendulum 170–179

calibration of system 172, 175

empowering the pendulum 170, 171

posing questions (to the pendulum) 176

preparing to dowse 172

uncertain responses 175, 176

E

Egil the Archer 25

Ehwaz 42, 140–141, 210, 218

Eightfold Wheel, the 51

Elder Futhark, the (original runic alphabet) 18, 59, 60, 88

Eostre (Easter) 81, 209, 210, 215

Erda (Mother Earth) 198

Erik the Red *20*, 21

Etruscan alphabet 14

F

Fehu 14, 18, 68–69, 193, 210, 218, 235

Five Directions Spread 49

Five elements (earth, air, fire, water, spirit) 218

Flibbertigibbet 29

Four directions, the 206, 207

Franks Casket, the *24*, *25*, 29

Frey 69, 89, 113, 141, 153

Freya 37, 69, 89, 113, 141

Frigg (Frigga or Fricka) 97, 121, 145, 206, 207

Futhark (see Runic Alphabet)

G

Gandr (runic wand) 192, 193, 204

  empowerment of the 204–205

  gandr magic 204–218

Gebo 25, 55, 92–93, 211, 218, 227

Gefjon 93

Gemini 141

Germania Cast 40

INDEX

Germanic tribes 13, 14, 15, 17, 18, 64

Gorm, King 29

Granby Runestone *57*

Gungnir, Odin's spear 206

H

Hagalaz 20, 100–101, 184, 208, 215, 218, 227

Hällristningar (rock carvings) *12*

Hanged Man, The (Tarot) 17, 21

Harold I (Harold Bluetooth) 29

Heimdall 89, 101, 125, 145, 161

Herodotus 13, 15

Hilddiguth's Stone 30, 31

Hrossketill's Stone 31

I

Iduna 17, 206

Ihwaz 55, 116–117, 209, 218, 230

Imbolc 209, 210, 215

Ing 37, 64, 85, 152, 153

Ingwaz 58, 152–153, 184, 210, 218, 227, 230

Invocations and prayers 37, 188, 193, 195, 197, 198, 200

Isa 25, 108–109, 209, 218, 227

Istaby Stone, the 30

J

Jarlabanke Runestones *26, 27, 231*

Jelling Stones, the 29

Jera 58, 112–113, 182, 183, 206, 209, 215, 218, 235

Jormungand, the world serpent 76

Jupiter 132, 145

K

Kalevala 21

Kauno 18, 88–89, 182, 184, 207, 211, 215, 218

Kylver Stone, the *14*

L

Laguz 148–149, 210, 215, 218

Lammas (see Lughnassad)

Leo 97

Libra 133

Litha 210, 215

Loki the Trickster 37, 76, 81

Lönnrot 21

Lughnassad(h) 211, 215

M

Mabon 211, 215

Magi, Adoration of the 25

Magic and mysticism, runes in 13, 14, 15, 21, 30

Man, Isle of 31

Mannaz 14, 25, 144–145, 210, 218, 235

Mars 77

Meanings of the runes 55, 58

converse and reverse meanings 58

Mercury 165

Mjöllnir, Thor's magic hammer 76, 193, 206

Monograms (see Bindrunes)

Moon, the 109, 149, 153, 157, 161

  phases of the 213, 215

Mother Holda (see Nerthus)

N

Naudiz 104–105, 208, 218, 227

Nerthus 85, 137, 149

Ninefold rule, the 205

Nine-Rune Cast, the 41

Nine Worlds of Yggdrasil 51

Njord 149, 207

Norns or Fates 101, 109, 206, 207

Norse language 13, 132, 222, 206, 207

Norse mythology 25, 51

Norsemen 18, 20, 31, 64, 76

Nyköping staff, the 30

O

Odin 17, 21, 37, 81, 93, 97, 145, 157, 164, 165

Odin's Rune Spread 43

Othila 156–157, 183, 210, 218

P

Perth 120–121, 209, 218

Pisces 93

Poetic Edda 25

Prose Edda 21

Q

Quest for Truth Spread

R

Ragnarok 76

Raido 14, 18, 84–85, 211, 218

Roman script 14, 25

Romulus and Remus 25

Rune fonts for computers 232, 233

computer graphics 235

Runes

  alphabet (see Runic alphabet)

  as a system of writing 12, 14, 15, 18

  drawing runes 234, 235

  incising of 15, 17

  interpreting the 54–165

  meanings of the 55, 58

    converse and reverse meanings 58

  methods of interpretation 40

  pronunciation of 20, 54, 55, 58

  reversible runes 42

    transcribing modern letters into 225

  writing using runes 222–235

Rune sets 21, 25 25, 36

Runestaff, the 204

Runic alphabet 12, 13, 14, 15, 18:

  Algiz 55, 124–125, 209, 215, 218

  Ansuz 18, 25, 55, 80–81, 164, 218, 230

  Berkanan 14, 40, 58, 65, 136, 137, 206, 210, 215, 218

INDEX

Dagaz 160–161, 184, 206, 210, 215, 218, 235

Ehwaz 42, 140–141, 210, 218

Fehu 14, 18, 68–69, 193, 210, 218, 235

Gebo 25, 55, 92–93, 211, 218, 227

Hagalaz 20, 100–101, 184, 208, 215, 218, 227

Ihwaz 55, 116–117, 209, 218, 230

Ingwaz 58, 152–153, 184, 210, 218, 227, 230

Isa 25, 108–109, 209, 218, 227

Jera 58, 112–113, 182, 183, 206, 209, 215, 218, 235

Kauno 18, 88–89, 182, 184, 207, 211, 215, 218

Laguz 148–149, 210, 215, 218

Mannaz 14, 25, 144–145, 210, 218, 235

Naudiz 104–105, 208, 218, 227

Othila 156–157, 183, 210, 218

Perth 120–121, 209, 218

Raido 14, 18, 84–85, 211, 218

Sowilo 128–129, 183, 184, 209, 218

Thurisaz 18, 76–77, 184, 215, 218, 227, 229, 230

Tiwaz 132–133, 182, 184, 210, 218, 227

Uruz 18, 72–73, 218

Wunjo 55, 96–97, 184, 208, 218runic

Runic associations and correspondences 64, 65

Runic Cross, the 45

Runic inscriptions
continuous-stave 30
tway-staved 31, 54

Runic pendulum (see Dowsing)

Runic relics and monuments 25–31

Runic wand (see Gandr)

S

Saga of Thidrik 25

Sagittarius 85

Samhain 208, 209, 215

Saturn 121

Scorpio 117

Scythia 12, 13, 14, 15, 222

Sigtuna runestones *22, 23*

Skuld the Norn 105, 206

Snivelling Corner 29

Sowilo 128–129, 183, 184, 209, 218

Sun, the 113, 129

T

Tacitus, Cornelius 15, 17

Tarot, The 17, 21, 45, 108

Tattoos (see Bindrunes)

Taurus 72

Tell, William 25

Thor 37, 72, 76, 77, 193, 206

Thor's Hammer Spread 50, 51

Three Lifetimes Spread 48, 49

Three-Rune Spread 43

Thurisaz 18, 76–77, 184, 215, 218, 227, 229, 230

Titus, the emperor 25

Tiw 37, 64, 132, 133, 206

Tiwaz 132–133, 182, 184, 210, 218, 227

U

Ullr 117

Urd, the Norn 72, 101, 206

Uruz 18, 72–73, 218

V

Vé, the (sacred rune-work area) 190, 192, 193, 204

 consecration of the Vé 193

 purification of the Vé 192, 195

Venus 81, 89

Verdandi, the Norn 109, 206

Vikings (see Norsemen) 76

Virgo 137

Volund, The Lay of (*Völundarkvida*) 25

W

Wayland the Smith 25, 29

Wayland's Smithy *28*, 29

Woods used for rune-making 25

World Tree, The (see Yggdrasil)

Wotan (see Odin)

Wunjo 55, 96–97, 184, 208, 218

Y

Yggdrasil, the World Tree 17, 21, 193

Younger Futhark 61

Yule 209, 215

Z

Zeus (see Jupiter, also Tiw)

ACKNOWLEDGEMENTS

© AA world Travel Library/TopFoto; pages 20, 97 © Alinari/
TopFoto; page 14 below © Arena PAL/TopFoto; page 206 ©
ARPL/HIP/TopFoto; pages 36, 144 below right © ArtMedia/
HipTopFoto; page 80 right © Bob Oswald; pages 12, 13 left, 14 top,
16, 17 both below, 20 left, 24 top, 29 top, 30 top, 31 all, 42 top, 60,
61 both, 65 below left, 68 below right, 69 right, 72 below, 76 below,
81, 85, 93 top, 101 top, 108 below left, 112 below, 121 top, 124 right,
141 below both, 148 below right, 149 below, 152 below right, 160
right, 170, 172, 179, 182 left, 183, 192, 194, 195, 204, 205, 207 left ©
The British Museum/Tip/TopFoto; page 24 below
©Campbell/TopFoto; pages 59, 88 top right, 94-95, 100 right, 109,
157 ©Caro/Bastian/TopFoto; pages 114-115, 153 © Caro/Hoffman
/TopFoto; page 209 below © Charlies Walker/TopFoto; pages 37, 73
left, 84 above, 92 below, 101 below, 117 top, 125 right, 133, 136 below,
141 top, 207 left © Classic Stock/TopFoto; page 113 © Derek
Mitchell/TopFoto; page 136 top right © Fortean/TopFoto; pages 29
below, 40, 46-47, 54 © Houghton/TopFoto; pages 4, 66-67 © John
Hedgecoe/TopFoto; pages 70-71, 102-103, 216-217 © Jon
Mitchell/TopFoto; pages 110-111 © Longhurst/TopFoto; pages 126-
127 © Lo Scarabeo; page 17 top, 108 right © Novosti/TopFoto page
65 top © Pedro Salaverria/TopFoto; page 64 © Peter Cairns/TopFoto;
pages 138-139 © Regency House Publishing Limited; front cover:
pages 2-3, 4, 5, 6, 7, 8-9, 18-19, 21, 32-33, 34, 42 below, 43, 44, 45, 48,
49, 50, 51 both, 52-53, 68 top, 72 top, 76 left, 80 left, 84 left, 88 left,
92 top, 96 top, 100 left, 104 left, 108 top, 112 top left, 116 left, 120
top, 124 left, 128 top, 132 top left, 136 top left, 140 left, 144 top, 148
below left, 152 below left, 156 top, 160 top left, 164 below, 168-169,
173, 174, 177, 178, 180-181, 182 right, 185, 188, 196, 199, 202-203,
220-221, 223, 224, 236-237 © Robert Piwko/TopFoto; page 112 right
© Roger-Viollet/TopFoto; page 58, 145 © Russ Bishop/Photri/
Topham/TopFoto; page 120 below right © TopFoto; page 28, 96

below, 129 right © Topham Picturepoint/TopFoto; page 15 top, 69
left, 89 © Ullsteinbild/TopFoto; page 35, 105 right © World Historic
Archive/TopFoto; page 13 right.

All of the following images supplied by Flickr Creative Commons:
Adrian Clark; page 190. Andrew Fogg; pages 78-79, 132 top right,
209 top. Alecin; page 208 below. Alexander Drachmann; page 223.
Alex Rouvin; page 132 below. Alfred Lui; page 171. Amy-b; page 140
right. B Mully; pages 118-119. Backpack Photography; pages 74-75.
Bluecoat: pages 162-163. Camille King; page 211 right.
Carly and Art; page 165. Carolin.Will; page 212. Chris Cardew; page
137 right. Chris Nichols; page 149 top. Corin Royal Drummond;
page 160 below left. Dave F; page 213. David Bacon; pages 146-147.
David Williams; page; 186. David Wilmot; pages 142-143. DH
Wright; page 156 below. eNil; page: 116 top Franco Folini; pages 150-
151. Frank Stevens; pages 130-131. Greg Westfall; page 210
Guldfisken; page 104 right. Ian Muttoo; pages 166-167. James
Jordan; page 129 left. Jarno; page 128 below, 137 left, 164 top. Jason
Hollinger; page 215 Jessica Merz; pages 158-159. Jim Champion;
pages 90-91, 134-135. Jim Clark; pages 154-155. Joe Shlabtnik; page
211 left. John Haslam: page 208 top. Ibrahim Lujaz; page 93 right.
Laszlo Ilyes; pages 98-99. Les Chatfield; page 121 below. Marieke
Knijjer; pages 22, 23, 26, 27, 56-57, 62, 63, 222, 226, 227, 231. Mark
Ordonez; page 117 below. Memotions; page 161. Michael Rhys; page
152 top Michelle Tribe; page 191. Micky; page 214. Milica Sekulic;
page 148 top. Missybossy; pages 82-83 Mwri; pages 106-107. Pablo
Gonzales; page 201. Pnjunction 2007; page 144 below left. Ross2085;
pages 38-39. Scot Campbell; pages 86-87. Steve Biehle; page 228.
Steve Jurvetson; page 219. Stormii80; page 200. Susan Williams; page
73 right.. WTL Photos; pages 122-123.

NOTES

NOTES

NOTES

NOTES

NOTES

NOTES

NOTES